2.99

Minister's
Worship
Handbook

Minister's Worship Handbook

by
James D. Robertson

BAKER BOOK HOUSE
Grand Rapids, Michigan

ISBN: 0-8010-7619-6

PHOTOLITHOPRINTED BY CUSHING - MALLOY, INC.
ANN ARBOR, MICHIGAN, UNITED STATES OF AMERICA
1974

To
Pauline

Contents

Foreword

The time is ripe for a book like this. This is particularly true in the evangelical world. Historically, evangelicals have been firm in their insistence upon the experience of corporate worship, and the author in this volume gives many helpful insights in this regard. In recent decades and perhaps during much of this century, however, the theological preoccupations of evangelicals have seemed to result in a less insistent attention being given to some of the characteristic historical precedents in evangelical worship.

In more recent years the phenomenal spiritual renewal, which has been taking place largely under evangelical auspices (and all of us thank God for it), has tended to exalt individuality above corporateness in worship. The emphasis upon each Christian "doing his own thing"—centering his attention upon his own experience and limiting his spiritual responsibility to giving his own witness—has certainly dimmed the appreciation for true corporate worship in many instances. It needs to be faced over and over again, especially in our day, that corporate worship is primarily "doing God's thing" together. As one writer recently noted, "The church must not substitute 'celebrating man' for worshiping God."

I trust that this book by my esteemed friend and colleague will receive a ready acceptance everywhere. It is filled with practical insights and guidelines for all who are sincerely concerned about the recovery of true worship in the contemporary Church.

The author has a high view of the nature of worship. He is truly in the Reformation—Evangelical tradition. He believes that worship is the true focus of the Church and that God is the true focus of worship. He declares that worship must not only make God real to the worshiper but also acclimate the worshiper to receiving and obeying God's revelation of truth and duty. The subjective elements in worship are not ignored. There is, however, an emphatic insistence upon a proper, proportionate balance between the objective and the subjective in worship.

This book also presents a wholesome and much-needed emphasis upon the significance of the minister in worship. The author affirms that the minister is the key to effective corporate worship. Once the minister understands his key role in this area he will sense his ethical responsibility both for keeping himself prepared spiritually and for his actual leadership in the service of worship.

The minister will keep himself spiritually prepared to be a leader in worship. Such preparation does not begin just a few hours before each worship service. It is a continuing endeavor, achieved through his daily devotional life and the dedicated fulfillment of all his ministerial activities. He lives with the sense of the holy. He recognizes the place of worship in the lives of those to whom he ministers because of his own need for worship.

The minister likewise gives attention in advance, under the inspiration of the Holy Spirit, to preparing for his leadership in each part of the worship service. He is concerned about the total worship service and its potential for spiritual influence upon the worshipers. He is always aware of both the privilege and the stewardship of his responsibility to lead the worshipers "up the altar stairs" into the very presence of God.

I commend this book to all Christians: to laymen, that they may gain a fuller understanding of the nature of worship and a deeper appreciation of the meaning of worship in Christian experience and activity; to ministers, that they may be aided in the discovery of guiding principles and the use of practical techniques for making worship more meaningful to all.

Frank Bateman Stanger
President
Asbury Theological Seminary

Acknowledgments

Abingdon Press for an extract from *A History of Evangelical Worship* by Ilion T. Jones, an extract from *The Burden of the Lord* by Ian MacPherson, two extracts from *Companion to the Book of Worship* by W. F. Dunkle, Jr. and J. D. Quillian, Jr. (editors); The Baptist Union of Great Britain and Ireland for three extracts from *The Reformation of Our Worship* by S. F. Winward; T. & T. Clark (Edinburgh) for two extracts from *Christian Worship in the Primitive Church* by A. B. Macdonald; James Clarke and Co., Ltd., for an extract from *The Transfigured Church* by John Henry Jowett; The Committee on Public Worship and Aids to Devotion of the Church of Scotland and Oxford University Press for seven prayers from the *Book of Common Order;* J. M. Dent and Sons, Ltd. and E. P. Dutton and Co., Inc. for an extract from *Essays and Addresses* by Frederick von Hugel; William B. Eerdman Publishing Co. for an extract from *History of Christian Worship* by Philip Schaff; Harper & Row for two extracts from *Worship, 1957* by Evelyn Underhill, three prayers from *Minister's Service Book* by James Dalton Morrison; Loeb Classical Library and Harvard University Press for an extract from *St. Augustine's Confessions;* The Macmillan Company for an extract from *The Way of Worship* by Scott Frances Brenner; The Macmillan Company of Canada, Macmillan (London and Basinstoke), and St. Martin's Press, Inc. for an extract from *Readings from St. John's Gospel* by William Temple; The Methodist Publishing House for three extracts from *The Christian Advocate* (June 20, 1963); Oxford University Press for two extracts from *Concerning Worship* by W. D. Maxwell, an extract from *Principles of Christian Worship* by Raymond Abba, two extracts from *The Word in Worship* by Thomas H. Keir, three extracts from *Worship: Its Theory and Practice* by J. J. Von Allmen; Prentice Hall, Inc. for an extract from *Word and Sacrament* by Donald Macleod; *Monday Morning* (a magazine for Presbyterian ministers) for an extract (February 1956); Charles Scribner's Sons for extracts from *Experience Worketh Hope* by Arthur John Gossip, *The Theology of the Sacraments* by Donald Baillie, *The Sense of the Presence of God* by John Baillie; The Society for the Promotion of Christian Knowledge for an extract from *The Office of the Ministry* by John Oman; *Theology Today* for an extract from Ernest Fuchs (October, 1962).

The author expresses his gratitude to President Frank B. Stanger for writing the Foreword and to Dr. Harold B. Kuhn for reading the manuscript and offering valuable suggestions.

James D. Robertson

11

1

The Nature of Worship

The Primary Objective of Christian Worship

God is the source and end of all true worship. Worship is the acknowledgement of the "worth-ship" (Anglo-Saxon, *weorthscipe*) of God. It is the human response to the divine nature. Worship begins with God. "When thou saidst, Seek ye my face; my heart said unto thee, Thy face, Lord, will I seek" (Ps. 27:8).

It is to be emphasized that man's response itself is divinely inspired: "No man can come to me, except the Father which hath sent me draw him" (John 6:44). If the Holy Spirit is the divine agent who motivates our worship, it is Christ who, by His finished work on Calvary, makes this motivation possible. Christ is the "Jacob's ladder" over which must pass all communication between man and God. Christ Himself is the dynamic of all His demands on life. Since it is God who creates the desire to worship and who brings about the response to grace, it can never be said that worship is an activity of man's merit.

Worship can rightly be offered only to God Himself. "Thou shalt worship the Lord thy God, and him only shalt thou serve" (Matt. 4:10). Worship is an end in itself. God is worthy of worship because of who He is.

Worship is offering. Throughout the Old Testament, to worship God was to present an offering that was always

13

symbolic of the offering of oneself. "Give unto the Lord the glory due unto his name: bring an offering, and come into his courts" (Ps. 96:8). Sacrifice was regarded as the sum of worship.

The priesthood of the New Covenant was established to the same end—to offer up spiritual sacrifices (I Peter 2:5). We go to church primarily to give, and secondarily, to receive. In worship we are to think of God first and of ourselves only in relation to God. It is of the very nature of worship for us to look away from ourselves to behold the reality of God and the spiritual world. True worship delivers from preoccupation with self.

The peak of Christian worship is adoration, such as that expressed in the seraphic hymn:

> Holy! Holy! Holy! is the Lord of hosts:
> The whole earth is full of His glory (Isa. 6:3).

"Such disinterested delight," says Evelyn Underhill, "is the perfection of worship."[1] It must not be thought, however, that this experience of self-effacing homage is reserved only for those souls who seem by nature best fitted to dwell in the rarefied atmosphere of the spiritual heights; for the command to love God with all one's heart is the divine standard for all men (Mark 12:30). One need not be a "Saint John of the Cross" or a "Saint Theresa" to experience the "wonder, love, and praise" that is evoked by the presence of God.

Let the Church be ever zealous in winning men; but its mission remains unfulfilled until it recognizes the need of cultivating in them the spirit of reverence and awe that leads to adoration, the most self-abnegating devotion of which man is capable. How else can the Church survive except through her vision of the glory of God! Is there in her life any other activity to compare with worship? Here is the vital spark of heavenly flame that is to inspire,

---

1. Evelyn Underhill, *Worship* (New York: Harper & Row, 1957), p. 5.

promote, and sustain the life of the soul. Here is the chain that is to bind mortal man to immortal God. Here is the door through which men enter, that they may apprehend something of the dimensions of both worlds. "I saw the Lord. . . ." said the prophet (Isa. 6:1). And what a vision was his of two worlds! It is the worship experience that charges the soul with the dynamic of God's presence, inspiring total response; and that invests the commonplace with a "light that never was seen on land or sea."

God's house is a place of revelation and response. We go to church to keep tryst with God: "And there I will meet with thee, and I will commune with thee . . ." (Exod. 25:22). Indeed the Church's only excuse for existence is in its providing a meeting place for God and man, a place where man can respond with all his heart and mind to the mystery, the majesty, and the mercy of God. No service is truly a worshipful service that does not make room for apprehension of these three. Short of this, a church may be a social institution, a center of religious discussion, or a mutual aid society—but it is not truly the Church. All too often we attend our places of worship, and nothing happens. We do not expect anything to happen. We go through the routine of ritual undisturbed by any realization of the presence of the Almighty. And we return to our tasks unrefreshed and unchallenged. We let ourselves be robbed of the very thing for which our hearts yearn. John Henry Jowett's remark to an earlier generation is still relevant:

> We leave our places of worship, and no deep and inexpressible wonder sits upon our faces. We can sing these lilting melodies; and when we get out into the streets, our faces are one with the faces of those who have left the theatres and music halls. There is nothing about us to suggest that we've been looking at anything stupendous and overwhelming. Far back in my boyhood I remember an old saint telling me that after some services he liked to make his way home alone by quiet bypaths, so that the hush of the Almighty might remain

on his awed and prostrated soul. That is the element we are losing.[2]

We are to come to church with the conviction that something will happen. The divine overtures are apprehended by him who enters God's house in the spirit of eager anticipation. The spirit of expectancy is essential to the very nature of worship.

Worship involves the whole man. Man's worship of God can never be divorced from man's moral and ethical content. God's self-disclosure is inextricably bound up with the life of righteousness. To the Hebrew prophet, righteousness was the essence of God's holiness. Worship apart from morality is something less than Christian. The qualification for fellowship with God is fitness for it. "Who shall ascend into the hill of the Lord? or who shall stand in his holy place? He that hath clean hands, and a pure heart; who hath not lifted up his soul unto vanity, nor sworn deceitfully" (Ps. 24:3-4). The true offering to God is righteousness of heart and life.

Worship in the New Testament also embraces obedience and service. "Why call ye me, Lord, Lord, and do not the things which I say?" (Luke 6:46). Our right response to God is at the heart of all true worship. As Arthur John Gossip says:

> Since He is here, and speaking to us, face to face, it is for us, in a hush of spirit, to listen for, and to, His voice, reproving, counseling, encouraging, revealing His most blessed will for us; and, with diligence, to set about immediate obedience. This and this, upon which He has laid His hand must go; and this and this to which He calls must be at once begun. And here and now I start to do it.[3]

---

2. John Henry Jowett, *The Transfigured Church* (London: James Clarke & Co., 1910), p. 22.
3. A. J. Gossip, *Experience Worketh Hope* (New York: Charles Scribner's Sons, 1945), pp. 24-25.

In the Bible there is no distinction between worship and service. Winward points out that the Hebrew verb "to serve" (*abhadh*) when used with reference to God includes every form of service, whether offered in temple worship or in daily life; and that in the New Testament the noun *leitourgia* (from which our word *liturgy* is derived) and the verb *leitourgein* are used without distinction between worship and service.[4]

The revelation of God is never one of His presence only; it is also one of purpose. "There can be no apprehension of the divine Presence that is not at the same time a summons to a divinely-appointed task." [5] The patriarchs and others who experienced visions of God were not only conscious of His presence but also informed concerning His purpose. Of Moses it is recorded, "And the angel of the Lord appeared unto him. . . . Come now, therefore and I will send thee unto Pharoah . . ." (Exod. 3:2, 10). Of Isaiah, "In the year that King Uzziah died I saw also the Lord sitting upon a throne. . . . Also I heard the voice of the Lord, saying, Whom shall I send . . . ?" (Isa. 6:1, 8). The spirit of true worship impels us to go about doing good, even as our Lord did. Some Christian churches might almost be monasteries for all the contact they have with the outside world.

If adoration includes worship, morality, and ethics, then obedience and service are not merely complementary to the worship experience. They are inherent in it.

For the Christian, worship is synonymous with life. It is no exercise for a "cloistered corner of the soul." It is the whole man who worships God. The comprehensiveness of worship is suggested by the late William Temple, Archbishop of Canterbury:

---

4. S. F. Winward, *The Reformation of our Worship* (London: Carey Kingsgate Press, 1964), p. 2.
5. John Baillie, *The Sense of the Presence of God* (New York: Charles Scribner's Sons, 1962), p. 206.

Worship is the quickening of conscience by God's holiness; the nourishment of mind with His truth; the purifying of imagination by His beauty; the opening of the heart to His love; the surrender of the will to His purpose; and all of this gathered up in adoration—the most selfless emotion of which our nature is capable, and therefore the chief remedy for that self-centeredness which is our original sin and the source of all actual sin.[6]

Inasmuch as man's ultimate response to God is measured in terms of offering, true worship is costly. Its chief end is the glory of God—an end that calls for the mobilization of all man's ransomed powers. Herein is the eternal paradox of the Christian religion: he that loses his life shall find it.

Subjective Relationships in Christian Worship. The subjective element is, of course, a part of all true worship. For worship is both an offering to God and a means of grace. If worship were altogether the outgoing of the soul in adoration, if it did not do something *to* and *for* the individual, Christian experience would soon become sterile. Worship is in its incipient stage when a man, finding himself in God's presence, experiences conviction, penitence, and confession. The vision of the awful perfection of the Creator over against the imperfection of the creature becomes the most effective source of conviction of sin. The vision enlightens, transforms, and purifies. Through public worship services and other means of grace, God continues His redemptive activity whereby souls are nourished and inspired. The psalmist sang: "Strength and beauty are in his sanctuary" (Ps. 96:6). Men come to church in part for the therapeutic values that the Christian faith has to offer. In these days of global storm and stress, many testify that were it not for the comfort and consolation of the Church they would be in danger of losing their sanity. The habit of

6. William Temple, *Readings in St. John's Gospel* (New York: Macmillan Co., 1947), p. 68.

churchgoing, of hearing the great saving truths of Christianity, helps us handle life with a heightened inner competence and a surer touch. However small our spiritual understanding, faith is stimulated, vision is clarified, and insight is deepened. Here the mind clears, the dust of confusion settles, and fears are allayed.

Public worship also provides the healing powers of Christian fellowship. The local church is a fellowship of believers. It is composed of men and women of kindred sympathies and aspirations who are joined into one because they are all joined to God and are partakers of the same Spirit. Because of this togetherness in worship, religious services on radio and television can never quite substitute for the individual's participation in the corporate worship of the local church.

Unity in common worship makes for adjustment in human relationships. Men, estranged from their fellows by selfishness, pride, envy, and indifference, have "come to themselves" in the worship setting. They have acquired a new understanding of the word *neighbor.*

Although there is a valid subjectiveness to worship whereby something redemptive and spiritually creative is happening to the worshiper, it needs to be emphasized that too much Protestant church worship seems to be almost entirely subjectively conceived. Too often it appears to be directed to the worshiper himself, concerned primarily with his personal gains and emotional satisfactions, and with seeking to influence his mental state. Too often it amounts to little more than an intellectual attentiveness that apprehends nothing of the divine presence. Its object is not the glory of God but the spiritual culture of the individual—a legitimate aim but a man-centered one. There is nothing wrong with seeking emotional or intellectual satisfactions or with desiring to be stirred to high resolve. But these motives must not be permitted to become the sole rationale in church worship. The center of attention in Christian worship is God, not the individual. "Devotion soon becomes petty and even cosy, turns back from self-oblation to self-consolation, where there is no acknowledgement of the august realities of faith."[7]

Finding a balance between the objective and the subjective aspects of worship constitutes a major problem in the worship of the Protestant church. It is basically the problem of sensing the reality of God—the miracle that should happen every time men gather for worship. "Surely the Lord is in this place . . . this is none other but the house of God, and this the gate of heaven" (Gen. 28:16-17).

Our theology of God conditions our worship perspective. For some, God is almost exclusively transcendent; for others He is altogether immanent. Man's nature calls for a sense of both the ultimate and the intimate. But when one is magnified at the expense of the other, religious experience is in danger of becoming either cold and legalistic or over-familiar and sentimental. The worship of God is a blend of both awe and love.

Worship—Essentially a Corporate Experience

It remains to be said that worship is fundamentally a corporate experience. It is the response of the Church, the Body of Christ, to God's mighty act of redemption in Jesus Christ. Worship is a family function. The individual approaches God as a member of Christ's Body. In the apostolic and primitive church, worship was "intensely corporate."[8] That worship is hollow which draws our souls into a splendid introspective isolation.

Much of today's worship is lacking in this awareness of corporateness in Christ. In many of our churches the most popular hymns are those stressing "I" and "me" rather than "we" and "us" in the God-man relationship. The

---

7. Underhill, *Worship,* p. 67.
8. Gregory Dix, *The Shape of Liturgy* (London: Dacre Press, 1945), p. 16.

corporateness of the worshiping body here on earth is reflected in I John 1:3: "That which we have seen and heard declare we unto you, that ye also may have fellowship with us: and truly our fellowship is with the Father, and with his Son Jesus Christ."

Since worship is communion between God and His people, the ministerial-centeredness of many prevailing patterns of Protestant worship is alien to its nature. In some churches, worship practices reflect a ministerial monopoly as much as does the Roman Mass. We need to keep in mind that the service of worship is the people's service. The worshipers are participators, not spectators. Not only are they to share in the hymns, prayers, and responses, but occasionally a lay member should be invited to assist in conducting the service, as for instance in the reading of the Scripture—a custom for which there is ancient precedent. Such lay participation bears testimony to the fact that leadership in public worship is not the exclusive privilege of men set apart by ordination.

To insist on the essentially corporate nature of worship is not to underestimate the value or necessity of private prayer. Corporate worship is not a substitute for private devotions. Indeed, the great masters of worship, those great spirits who live in the heights, tell us that the life of personal devotion is "the first essential of the Christian." Each life lived in personal fellowship with God makes its indispensable contribution to that total response that is the essence of worship.

We are to remember, moreover, that our worship is never just the offering of the local congregation. We are no body of isolated worshipers. We come before God as members of a great family, a part of the communion of saints both on earth and in heaven. In worship, the Church militant joins with the Church triumphant and all the host of heaven.

> "Therefore with angels and archangels and with all the company of heaven, we laud and magnify Thy glorious Name."

2

Historical Backgrounds

The Temple

The beginnings of Christian worship are to be found in the Temple and the synagogue. The true center of Israel's worship was the Temple. There within the Holy of Holies God was believed to dwell, in a manner completely beyond man's comprehension. To the Hebrew mind the idea of a Holy God, with its implications of mystery, transcendence, and moral majesty, was dreadful to contemplate. The dark emptiness of this most sacred place could only suggest the awfulness of the divine presence.

Within the Holy of Holies rested the ark of the covenant, symbol of God's presence. It was a rectangular box made of acacia wood and covered with gold, its lid, or "mercy seat," overshadowed by cherubim with outstretched wings. The whole was fashioned according to the pattern given to Moses on the mount (Exod. 25:10ff.). The ark contained the two tablets of the Decalogue (Exod. 25:16, 21; 40:20; Deut. 10:1-5), a pot of manna, and Aaron's rod (Heb. 9:45). It served as a meeting place where God revealed His will to His servants (Exod. 25:22; 30:36; Lev. 16:2; Josh. 8:6). Only the high priest might enter the Holy of Holies, and that on just one day of the year—the Day of Atonement. For another to have done so at any time would have meant instant death. On that day the high priest, passing within the veil separating the Holy Place from the Holy of Holies, sprinkled the blood of the sin-offering on the mercy seat (Lev. 16:2, 14), a symbolic act that found its fulfillment in Christ, our great High Priest, who, as the author of the Epistle to the Hebrews assures us, by His blood, the blood of the everlasting covenant, made possible our access into the holiest.

Notwithstanding his belief in the divine omnipresence, the Israelite saw God's presence as severely localized. All his worship was directed toward the Holy of Holies in the Temple. Even during the period of the Exile, synagogues were commonly built so that worship was centered at one and the same time toward Jerusalem and the ark.

Temple worship was a highly symbolic ritual—in substance, a common acknowledgement of the sovereignty of God. Its main emphasis was sacrificial, an emphasis that was to find its culmination in Christ's sacrifice of Himself. Many priests participated in the temple sacrifices, always offered in a context of elaborate symbolism and ritual. Two services were held daily; one at daybreak, the other at sunset. Almost the same order of worship obtained for both services. After the offering of incense, an unblemished lamb was sacrificed. Next, formal prayers were recited, including the saying of the Shema (Deut. 6:4-9; 11:13-21; Num. 15:37-41). Following a sacrifice of praise, the service closed as it began—with the offering of incense.

The contribution of the Temple to worship in the Christian Church is in the realm of idea. In Christian worship we use the same basic concepts. From the Temple were carried over such terms as sacrifice, atonement, lamb, repentance, high priest, white robes, and bread and wine.

The Synagogue

It is commonly believed that the synagogue (Greek, "assembly") arose during the period of the Babylonian captivity (6 B.C.) as a direct response to the collapse of temple services. Although the synagogue had no altar and no sacrifice, its services were synchronized with the temple sacrifices so that those worshiping could by intention identify themselves with the worship of the Temple. The temptation to regard the worship of the synagogue as a corrective to that of the Temple must be resisted. As one authority points out:

> In the full religious practice of the devout Jew of New Testament times, both Temple and Synagogue were accepted as the two aspects of the total response to God: as the moral demands of the prophets, and the ritual demands of the Law, were accepted without any sense of incongruity.[1]

The furnishings of the synagogue were reminiscent of the Temple. The focal point of worship was the ark, which housed the scrolls of the Law and the Prophets. It corresponded, in part at least, to the Holy of Holies. It, too, was separated by a veil. Likewise in the synagogue, in front of the veil rested the ceremonial lampstand, its light burning perpetually. The ark commonly faced the entrance of the building. Before it and facing the worshipers were the "chief seats" of the rulers of the synagogue. From a platform near the middle, the service was conducted.

Some liturgical elements were carried over from the temple service, particularly the use of certain psalms, the recitation of the Decalogue and the Shema, and some very old prayers. Distinctive of synagogue worship was the large place given to the reading and exposition of Scripture and to prayer. If temple worship emphasized God's sovereignty, the synagogue service stressed devotion to the Law.

The synagogue community was governed by the elders, who no doubt elected the ruler of the synagogue from among themselves. This official, although responsible for the conduct of the service, did not himself actively lead

---

1. Evelyn Underhill, *Worship* (New York: Harper & Row, 1957), p. 20.

but delegated the various tasks to others. Laymen were the active agents of the worship: they customarily read the Scriptures, led the prayers, and brought the address. On the Sabbath, at least seven persons took their turn in reading from the Law passages for the day. There was but one reading from the Prophets, whose writings were considered less sacred than the Law. Although a rather severe ritual eventually governed the service, it left room for a measure of freedom, such as in selecting the lessons, in the sermon, and in the question period permitted the congregation at the close of the address.

If the Temple passed on the basic concepts of our Christian worship, the synagogue set the general pattern of the service. The worship of the Christian Church, like that of the synagogue, includes Scripture reading, exposition of the Word, prayer, and certain liturgical acts such as standing for prayer and the saying of responsive Amens. Although there is no recorded instance of singing in the synagogue service, it is entirely possible that the Psalms, long identified with temple worship, were sung.

The New Testament Church

Although the writers of the New Testament are for the most part silent concerning the worship practices of their times, they leave the impression that corporate worship among the first Christians was characterized by a certain irrepressible vitality and spontaneity. It is surely a mistake to refer to this spiritual exuberance as a transient feature of New Testament Christianity, as though in the end human nature must inevitably conform to a set pattern. The worship of these early Christians was primarily of the spirit, conducted within the framework of simple and familiar forms.

It seems evident that in these first Christian gatherings the Holy Spirit was manifest in great power, affecting every part of worship: the singing, praying, preaching, witnessing, and giving. We cannot really catch the spirit of these early Christians until we approach it in terms of their experience; that is, from within:

> Within them dwelt a surging of new thought and emotion; the most astounding things had happened to them; a deep thankfulness and an irrepressible joy possessed them; and their worship came from them much as its full-throated song comes from a bird—as the simple, spontaneous overflowing expression of an exuberant life that must of necessity have an outlet.... It was *objective* worship in the sense that the worshiper's mind became habituated to an objective poise—to an adoring, contemplative gaze, directed, not inward, but outward; and it was objective worship also in the deeper sense that it was believed to accomplish something actual between man and God.[2]

Communion with the risen Christ, especially associated with the breaking of bread, was the chief motive in the worship of these early disciples. They met in the firm conviction of the continuing real and intimate presence of their living Lord. Had He not promised, saying, "Where two or three are gathered together in my name, there am I in the midst of them" (Matt. 18:20)?

Simplicity seems to have been the keynote of this worship. It is to be expected that the Jewish Christian service was compounded of some of the main elements of synagogue worship, including the reading and expounding of the Scriptures and the recital of prayers. That hymns were also added may be inferred from several New Testament passages (e.g., Eph. 5:19, Col. 3:16; and from hymn fragments found in Eph. 3:21, I Tim. 3:16, II Tim. 2:11-13; Rev. 4:8 and 5:9ff.).

That worship in New Testament times was flexible, providing for the needs of widely differing communities and people, may be inferred from Paul's writing to the Gentile Christian church at Corinth. The synagogue tradition seems to have had little influence upon this church

2. A. B. Macdonald, *Christian Worship in the Primitive Church* (Edinburgh: T. & T. Clark, 1934), pp. 2-3, 9.

with its "high valuation of spontaneity and enthusiasm, glossalalia and direct revelation."[3] Its worship provided largely for the manifestation of the Spirit through individual members of the congregation. "To sum up, my friends: when you meet for worship, each of you contributes a hymn, some instruction, a revelation, an ecstatic utterance . . . " (I Cor. 14:26. NEB.).

Absence of a norm in New Testament worship does not mean that the services were conducted without definite pattern or that they were at the mercy of mood or desire. "Free" worship, rightly understood, does not imply disorder or worship necessarily detached from traditional forms. If the New Testament church recognized the value of free, charismatic expression in its worship, it was not unmindful of the fact that this liberty carried with it also an element of restraint. Worship evoked by the Spirit is always in harmony with the revelation of Christ as contained in the Word. "The spirits of the prophets are subject to the prophets" (I Cor. 14:32). Paul, seeking to correct abuses in the worship of the Corinthian church, set forth a few principles for guidance. "Let all things be done unto edifying. . . . God is not the author of confusion, but of peace. . . . Let all things be done decently and in order" (I Cor. 14:26, 33, 40).

Primitive Christian worship was held in private homes (cf., Rom. 16:5; I Cor. 16:19; Col. 4:15; Philem. 2). It was not public in the sense that it was open to all comers. On the contrary, it was recognized as a highly private activity, peculiar to the group of believers. There was no organization, strictly speaking, binding the "house churches" together. Paul's earliest statement concerning the emergence of leaders in the church is in I Corinthians 12:28, where he speaks of God's having chosen "first apostles, secondarily prophets, thirdly teachers. . . ."

There was an element of New Testament worship, how-

---

3. S. F. Winward, *The Reformation of Our Worship* (London: Carey Kingsgate Press, 1964), pp. 100-101.

ever, that did not derive from either the Temple or the synagogue. The sacrament of the Lord's Supper was distinctively Christian in its origin and significance. It is hardly germane to our interests to discuss the question whether the last supper that our Lord took with His disciples was the Passover or a supper of sanctification held weekly in preparation for the Sabbath by small groups of male Jews, possibly the *Kiddush* meal. The Synoptic writers clearly state that it was the former (cf., Mark 14:12). John, however, says that after the supper had ended and Jesus was on trial, His accusers did not go into the judgment hall that they might not be defiled "but might eat the passover" (John 18:28b). It is entirely possible that the Synoptic writers regarded the supper of sanctification as an inseparable part of the Passover.

In the primitive Church, the Supper, or the Eucharist as it came to be called, was observed every Sunday morning, the day commemorating our Lord's resurrection—the "Lord's Day." It was celebrated before or at daybreak, the hour associated with Christ's triumph over the grave. It was not conceived as a solemn wake, held in mournful remembrance of Him who died. "From the beginning it was a meal of fellowship dominated by thanksgiving and offered in praise, wonder, and adoration of the Lord of life who had broken the bonds of death and was alive for evermore with His people."[4] Untroubled by theories of His presence that were to divide the Church of a later age, these first disciples nevertheless knew that presence to be a reality. It is unlikely that they believed it to be localized in the elements, which to them were undoubtedly less the occasion of His presence than a part of the total act of the worshiper's grateful remembrance and prayerful communion with the risen Lord.

In the New Testament Church, certain worship practices

---

4. W. D. Maxwell, *Concerning Worship* (London: Oxford University Press, 1949), p. 14.

flourished but for a season. One of these was the communal meal. Inasmuch as fellowship meals were common among both Jews and Gentiles, it was natural that the members of the new "sect" should adopt the practice. Christians gathered in the home of one of their number, each family bringing food to be shared in common, with special concern for the poor and the widows of the Christian community. This "love feast," or "agape," suggests to us the warmth and inward depths of the fellowship that existed among the early Christians. By the time of Paul's writing to the Corinthians (ca. A.D. 55), it is evident that the church at Corinth was in the habit of engaging in a common meal prior to partaking of the Lord's Supper (I Cor. 11:17-34). From the apostle's strictures against this church, we know that in the observance of the meal, abuses had arisen to make its continuance undesirable.

Speaking in tongues was yet another element of New Testament worship that proved to be impermanent, notwithstanding its reappearance from time to time in the life of the Church. Paul criticized the misuse of the practice (cf., I Cor. 14:19). The phenomenon as it appeared in his day was evidently not the same as that which happened on the Day of Pentecost (i.e., speaking in foreign languages) but was a kind of ecstatic outburst uninterpretable to both speaker and hearer. Nevertheless the primitive Church did see in it a divine gift peculiar to some believers. Paul discouraged the Corinthians from seeking this gift, urging them rather to cultivate gifts that edify.

The First Christian Centuries

During the first two centuries, the liturgy of the Church was undoubtedly comparatively simple. The few available sources of information suggest as much. The first complete description of the Sunday service appears in Justin Martyr's *First Apology,* written about A.D. 150. The service was composed of two parts: the first consisted of Scripture

readings, an exhortation, and prayers; the second com-
prised the observance of the Lord's Supper. Dom Gregory
Dix, who has done extensive research in Christian worship
in these early centuries, concludes that by the third and
fourth centuries public worship consisted of these two
parts. The first, harking back to the synagogue, was largely
instructional, and was preparatory to the second. There is
no evidence that the first part constituted a service by
itself. But only those persons admitted into the full fellowship of the Church were permitted to remain for Communion. Justin's account represents in broad outline the
structure of the Christian worship service that remains to
this day in every historic liturgy, and in all branches of the
Christian Church:

> On Sunday a meeting of all, who live in cities and villages, is
> held, and a section from the Memoirs of the Apostles and the
> writings of the Prophets is read, as long as time permits. When
> the reader has finished, the president, in a discourse, gives an
> exhortation to the imitation of those noble things. After this
> we all rise in common prayer. At the close of the prayer, bread
> and wine with water are brought. The President offers prayer
> and thanks for them, according to the power given him, and
> the congregation responds the Amen. Then the consecrated
> elements are distributed to each one, and partaken, and are
> carried by the deacons to the houses of the absent. The
> wealthy and the willing then give contributions according to
> their free will, and the collection is deposited with the presi-
> dent, who therewith supplies widows and orphans, poor and
> needy, prisoners and strangers, and takes care of all who are in
> want. We assemble in common on Sunday, because this is the
> first day, on which God created the world and the light, and
> because Jesus Christ our Saviour on the same day rose from
> the dead and appeared to his disciples.[5]

The Middle Ages

About the beginning of the fifth century, Christian
worship had passed from a more or less fluid state to one

---

5. Philip Schaff, *History of the Christian Church* (Grand Rapids:
Wm. B. Eerdmans, 1960), pp. 223-224.

of fixed forms. For the next thousand years and more the Church was to live through a desolate night of the soul, its spiritual flame vastly dimmed by error and superstition. In the West there were two rites: the Roman, deriving from the church at Rome; and the Gallican, controlling the Western World outside of Rome. The Roman rite in the beginning was simple. It was the Mass reduced to its least possible expression. The origin of the Gallican liturgy remains obscure. But many of its elements point to an oriental derivation. In expression it was ornate and colorful—the consequence of natural development among a semibarbarian people. As the church at Rome grew more powerful, it eventually suppressed the Gallic rite, but not before much of it had been absorbed into the Roman Mass.

The following are some of the evidences of the decline of public worship in the Middle Ages:

> The common man was denied the right of individual approach to God.

> The Mass came to be regarded as an objective sacrifice repeating or continuing the work of Calvary. It was believed that at the consecration of the elements the bread and wine were miraculously transformed into the actual body and blood of Christ (transubstantiation), to be offered anew in the Mass. No longer was the occasion that of a simple supper, symbolic of the fellowship of the believers with their risen Lord and with one another. The supper had developed into a dramatic spectacle in which the worshipers were spectators rather than participators. Instead of weekly Communion the laity eventually partook only once a year.

> The Scriptures were practically inaccessible to the people.

> The sermon fell into serious decline, and moral instruction all but disappeared.

> Congregational singing was discontinued.

> Worship was no longer conducted by the leader facing the people from behind the table, as was the custom in the beginning. The table had become an altar set against the wall

of the apse, the priest performing his liturgical acts facing the altar and with his back to the people.

The service was everywhere said in Latin, an alien tongue.

The people were exploited by paid masses and indulgences. Prayers for the dead became urgently important, and a price was exacted for their repetition.

Since only a priest could offer sacrifice, the prestige of the priesthood was inordinately enhanced. It often happened, moreover, that priests, victims of their own system, became mercenary and tyrannical, using their power to enrich the Church at the expense of the spiritual welfare of the people.

The Reformation

The efforts of the Reformers to recover for the Christian Church the doctrines and worship practices of primitive Christianity met with substantial gains. Worship again became rational and intelligible. To the common man was restored the right to approach God directly, without benefit of the priesthood. The Scriptures were translated into the vernacular tongues. Preaching came into its own, and congregational singing was reinstated.

Basic to these gains was the repudiation of the Roman Mass as an objective sacrifice. The Mass again became "The Supper of the Lord," of which all were made partakers. The Communion table was removed from against the wall in the apse, the minister conducting the service from behind it and facing the people.

The reaction against Rome, however, was not without its attendant excesses and failures. Bitterness toward the Mass led for a time to the displacement of Communion as the supreme act of worship. Many fine old churches, priceless works of art, and centuries-old liturgical treasures were needlessly destroyed as the fury of the Reformation sympathizers gained momentum.

Because, moreover, the Reformers were inescapably the

offspring of their times, they inherited the individualism and clericalism of the medieval Church, a legacy responsible in part at least for the ministerial domination of the Protestant service to this day. The minister continued to read the Scriptures, offer the prayers, preach the Word, and administer the Sacraments, with little or no assistance. Notwithstanding the recovery of the great doctrine of the priesthood of all believers, the role of the congregation continued for the most part to be one of passive assimilation rather than active participation.

Of the two Reformers, Luther was more conservative toward change in worship practice. He was tolerant of historic rites and ceremonies that were not forbidden by the Scriptures. On the whole, the Lutheran churches experienced little change; altars, vestments, shrines and pictures, and even crucifixes were retained. Calvin, on the other hand, demanded abolition of everything that was not expressly enjoined in the Bible. Worship, he insisted, must come from the heart, independent of set forms. It is interesting to note that Calvin's influence on Protestant worship has far exceeded Luther's. Although the Baptists, Methodists, Congregationalists, and Disciples of Christ did not completely accept Calvin's theology, each of these bodies has for the most part conformed to the Presbyterian way of worship.

It was the intention of both Luther and Calvin to restore the emphasis that they believed the Church in the beginning placed upon the Word and the Lord's Supper. To them the two parts constituted an organic whole. Both men called for weekly celebration of the Supper. Luther's insistence on this met with much success; for the Lutheran churches in Germany observed Communion weekly well into the eighteenth century. Calvin's failure in this regard was due to opposition from the civil authorities in Geneva, who limited Communion to four times a year. Zwingli, who did not feel that the Supper was necessary to every worship service, and who regarded it primarily as a confessional act, was content with quarterly communion, a practice that was to be largely followed in England and Scotland, and which resulted in making the sermon the climax of the service.

3

Setting and Symbol in Worship

The Setting

It is true that the sincere soul may find God anywhere. The divine presence is not limited to places, times, or seasons. For purposes of corporate worship, however, a designated time and place must be agreed upon. Public worship is representative, not exclusive. As the late William Temple said:

> We set apart places as sacred, not to mark other places as profane, but to represent and remind us of the sanctity of all places. We set apart certain times as sacred, not to mark other times as secular, but to represent and remind us of the sanctity of all time.[1]

We cannot ignore the fact that in Old Testament times God gave meticulous instructions concerning the building of the place in which He was to be worshiped, and that, when finished, it was a thing of beauty. With some, however, beauty is suspect; but not without reason. Too often, religion has deteriorated by being submerged in the aesthetic element. Nonetheless God meant art to be the handmaid of religion. That the worship setting influences the character of the worship, cannot be gainsaid. The place

---

1. William Temple, *Christus Veritas* (London: Macmillan Co., 1949), p. 242.

does not determine the reality of His presence, but it may help prepare the heart for the realization of that presence. The architecture of the church, the interior arrangement, and the furnishings—even if reduced to a bare minimum—all may help or hinder worship. The worship setting should as much as possible suggest a place "where prayer is wont to be made." Simplicity, restraint, and dignity should characterize the whole.

The traditional worship setting calls for either the chancel or the center pulpit plan.

The Chancel Arrangement

The first exclusively Christian gatherings, it will be recalled, were held in private homes. Paul sent greetings through Philemon to "the church in thy house" in Colossae. As Christianity moved westward, meetings were held in basilicas, buildings commonly used as Roman law courts and as public assemblies. The basilica, which became the pattern for the great churches of the age of Constantine, was originally a rectangular structure, its length about three times its width. By the second century, basilican-type buildings had been erected for purposes of Christian worship. At one end, in the form of a half-circle, was the apse, which contained a platform where the judges formerly sat. In using the basilica for public worship, it was but natural for the leaders of the service to occupy the apse, leaving the central portion of the building for the people. This main part became known as the "nave" (from the Latin *navis,* a ship, to which the Church was often likened). The apse was eventually replaced by a simple rectangular addition, the "chancel." The word is a Latin derivative signifying "lattice" or "crossbar." The chancel was enclosed by lattices to indicate that it was an area reserved for the priests in the performance of their holy task, an arrangement reminiscent of Old Testament models of the tabernacle and the Temple. Because it was regarded

as the holiest part of the church, the chancel was also
known as the "sanctuary," a designation that obtains in
most Roman churches to this day.

In the typical Anglican church the chancel contains the
choir, the communion rail, and beyond the rail the sanctuary. In the sanctuary area rests the altar, in an elevated
position, set against the wall as in the medieval church.
Below it on the lower chancel floor on either side are the
choir stalls. At the front, on the same level, are the pulpit
and the lectern. The chancel choir is inherited originally
from the monastic chapels, in which the monks' stalls
faced one another. The revival of the chancel choir is
attributed to the Oxford Movement in Britain. In the
ancient church, the choir was located in a front section of
the nave, whereas in the medieval church it sang from a
gallery in the back.

Chancel arrangement commonly reflects theological emphasis. Since Protestant Christianity holds the revelation of
the Word to be the foundation of the Christian faith, it
considers the Word central in the total act of worship.

> At its heart is the divine self-giving. That is precisely what
> the Reformers meant by the Word of God, not just a word
> about God, or even a message from God. The Word is nothing
> less than the self-communication of God—God coming to us,
> meeting us in judgment and in mercy, imparting Himself to us
> in redeeming love; what Oscar Cullman calls God in His revela-
> tory action.[2]

In public worship, the Word is communicated in two
ways: in the written and spoken Word (in Scripture and in
sermon) and in the sacraments. Pulpit, lectern, and table
are not to be taken as three separate symbols but as three
facets through which the Word of God is proclaimed.
Today there is among Protestants a strong tendency

---

2. Raymond Abba, *Principles of Christian Worship* (London: Oxford University Press, 1957), p. 45.

toward some form of chancel set-up that gives due recognition to pulpit, lectern, table, and baptismal font.

A chancel arrangement that suggests separation between minister and people is hardly in keeping with the tenets of evangelical theology. It is surely a dubious practice, moreover, to speak of the chancel or any part of it as the "sanctuary," as though one part of God's house were holier than another. Whatever the architectural design in the front area of the church, it should bear clear witness to the fact of the priesthood of all believers—to the right of every man to approach God for himself—that glorious inheritance restored to us at the time of the Protestant Reformation. In the early Church, the leader, when observing Communion, stood behind the table, facing the people, with no rail between. If a rail separates chancel from people, it may well have a center opening symbolizing the people's free access to the Communion table. In Western Europe, the table was free-standing until the eleventh century, when it was pushed back against the wall to the position formerly occupied by the "cathedra" of the bishop.[3] The Reformers restored it to its original place. In the stress of the present liturgical revival, it is to be observed that while many Protestant churches are transforming the table into an altar set against the wall, there is a trend in the Church of Rome to project the altar into the nave. In bringing it nearer the people, the hope is that congregational participation in the Mass will be more intimate.

The table in evangelical Protestantism should not be elevated above the pulpit; nor is it to be set against the wall. It should be free-standing, usually in the back-center, or, in a deeper chancel, nearer the front. Behind the table, in the chancel arrangement, there is likely to be an ornamental screen (*reredos*) or a curtain (*dossal*) hanging from the wall.

---

3. J. J. von Allmen, *Worship: Its Theology and Practice* (New York: Oxford University Press, 1965), p. 258.

The table should look like a table. An altar suggests sacrifice, and Protestants reject the idea that the sacrament of the table is itself a sacrifice. Jones voices concern at the widespread use in Protestant circles of the terms "altar" and "altar-table":

> One wonders if they have forgotten the real issues of the Reformation and the 'rock from whence they were hewn.' . . . To retransform the table into a high altar, separated from and above the people and the Word of God, is a complete betrayal of the evangelical faith.[4]

In the early Church, the only things deemed worthy to be placed on the table were the Communion vessels.[5] What need of more? Why not let this venerable symbol of God's fellowship with man rest unadorned in its own strength? Who can add to it or take away?

In the early Christian centuries, the service was conducted from behind the table. This position (the "basilican posture") is the more primitive. Although in many Protestant churches where the table is in the apse and free-standing, the minister customarily leads the service from the lectern or pulpit; or he may conduct it from behind the table, proceeding to the lectern for the Scripture readings and to the pulpit during the singing of the hymn before the sermon. If the table is in the form of an altar attached to the wall, the minister usually conducts the service from the pulpit or lectern; or he may lead it standing at the "north" end of the table.

The Center Pulpit Arrangement

In the churches of the Reformed faith, the pulpit long occupied a central position, a custom derived from the Reformation, which emphasized the reading and preaching

---

4. Ilion T. Jones, *A Historical Approach to Evangelical Worship* (New York: Abingdon Press, 1954), p. 230.
5. Gregory Dix, *The Shape of the Liturgy* (London: Dacre Press, 1945), p. 419.

of the Word as the basis of Christian faith. In this arrangement, the table rested in front of the pulpit and on the congregational level. The service was conducted from the pulpit, the minister moving to the table for the dedication of the offering. The Communion ritual, of course, was always read from the table.

The lower level was not intended to imply subordination of the sacrament to preaching. The table stood on this level, symbolically in the midst of the people, to demonstrate the fact of the priesthood of all believers. Free-standing and thus located, it also defined the Church as "the fellowship of believers gathered about the Lord's table in response to the Lord's command."[6]

Although the side pulpit of the chancel plan succeeds in making the minister less conspicuous, the pulpit-centered arrangement need not make the worship service unduly man-centered. If the preacher is truly God's man, this objection can hardly be sustained. It is entirely possible to overstate the case for either the table-centered or pulpit-centered worship setting. If the young minister finds himself in a setting that is incongruous with his religious tradition or beliefs, he will remember that the God he worships is bigger than the interior arrangement of the church. God is not bound by ecclesiastical design. It cannot be said that He is more present in one kind of setting than in another. People of all generations and in all kinds of worship environments—Gothic cathedral and windswept hillside—can testify alike to the reality of His presence in the experience of public worship. When all is said and done, the truly evangelical spirit is reflected in William Cowper's splendid hymn:

> Jesus, where'er Thy people meet,
> There they behold Thy mercy-seat:
> Where'er they seek Thee, Thou art found,
> And every place is hallowed ground.

6. Scott Francis Brenner, *The Art of Worship* (New York: Macmillan Co., 1961), p. 11.

For Thou, within no walls confined,
Inhabitest the humble mind.

SYMBOL IN WORSHIP

Since man is not pure spirit but very much a creature of the senses, spiritual communication between God and man is possible only through symbols. A symbol is that which can be apprehended by the senses but which stands for something that cannot be sensibly perceived. Symbolism is of the nature of poetry. Poetry is truth, even if it does not speak with mathematical preciseness. It suggests infinitely more than it can say, for it represents that which transcends man's mind. In His dealings with men, God often spoke through symbol—be it rainbow, brazen serpent, altar, tabernacle, temple, bread and wine, or word.

In describing God, the Biblical writers are confined to expressions such as "dwelling in unapproachable light" (I Tim. 6:16, NEB); He "walketh upon the wings of the wind" (Ps. 104:3); and He is "the fountain of living waters" (Jer. 2:13). Biblical language about spiritual realities is rich in metaphorical, spatial symbolism: "The Lord is in his holy temple" (Hab. 2:20); "He that dwelleth in the secret place of the most High shall abide under the shadow of the Almighty" (Ps. 91:1); "In my Father's house are many mansions" (John 14:1). Jesus engaged in symbolic acts: He prostrated Himself in prayer (Mark 14:35); lifted up His eyes to heaven (John 11:41; 17:1; Mark 6:41); was baptized (Mark 1:9); broke bread (Mark 6:41, 7:6, 14:22); and lifted up His hand in blessing (Mark 24:50). Jesus taught that natural objects could speak sacramentally to us, nourishing our faith and imparting comfort: "Behold the fowls of the air . . ."; "Consider the lilies of the field. . . ." His primary symbolism was the expression "the kingdom of heaven"; it was the theme of His preaching (Matt. 4:17).

If it is true that symbols are necessary to man's worship,

it is also true that no one symbol is always unavoidably indispensable. Many ancient symbols have fallen into disuse, such as the kiss of peace and the raising of the hands in prayer. Even the few symbols that most Christians feel to be highly significant—because Christ commanded their use—cannot be said to be absolutely indispensable to salvation. For instance, under certain circumstances, both the Protestant and the Roman branches of the Church make provision for dispensing with the Sacraments.

Historically, Protestantism has never made extensive use of symbols. The Reformers were cautious here. Believing that the prime appeal in worship is to the mind, they favored verbal symbols, like the reading and preaching of the Word, rather than sensory symbols, like statuary and incense. When Christianity appeals to the senses more than to the intellect, spiritual life is in grave danger of becoming impoverished.

It is not enough that Christian symbols be in accord with theological belief; they must also be meaningful to the people. They should first of all make one think of God and evoke reverence. In evangelical worship, basic eye-symbols are the Bible, the pulpit and the lectern, the Communion table and baptismal font, and the empty Cross.

Discreet use of symbolic action can make a vital contribution to the service. In the Scottish churches it has long been the practice for the beadle (a minor church officer) to bear the Bible to the pulpit before the entrance of the minister. This act, which dramatizes the significance of the Word, is reminiscent of the removal of the sacred scroll from the ark in the synagogue service and also of the "Little Entrance" in the worship service of the undivided Church, when the clergy bore the Scriptures into the chancel or to the "ambon" in the nave. In the church service, the "Little Entrance" represented one of the two high points in the liturgy. The other climax, the "Great

Entrance," consisted of the offertory, or the reception of bread and wine and the placing of them on the altar.

Other symbolic actions are familiar to us, such as standing to sing, kneeling or bowing to pray, walking to the front of the church to make public confession of faith, and processionals and recessionals. In evangelical worship—all symbolic action should be confined to simple, meaningful movements.

4

Order in Worship

No group meeting regularly for worship can dispense with the matter of ritual, for worship must be embodied in form. Ritual is simply an accustomed way of doing things. It is part of every kind of group activity—the social gathering, the committee meeting, or the ball game. If men are to do things together, there must be general agreement on procedure. The form that worship takes may vary according to time and place. The worship of the fourth century differed at many points from that of the ninth, while again the worship of the churches in Asia Minor differed from that of the church of Egypt. But these variations did not necessarily compromise the basic unity of the Christian faith.

Unordered worship may easily become disordered and extravagant. All too often it leaves the congregation at the mercy of the preacher's temperament or mood. It was Martin Luther who said that the people ought to be protected against a parson by a liturgy. He who is always seeking variety in the service may continue for a time with improvisations and with constantly changing forms, but before long the quest for novelty will exhaust itself. The service that is conducted in a way that keeps the congregation guessing can hardly be expected to promote reverent thinking. "The formality of informality is the greatest formality." Then there is a kind of "free" worship that amounts to little more than doing the same thing in the same way Sunday after Sunday.

It is never primarily a question of more or less ritual. Worship is never spiritual simply because it follows no order or pattern; it is never empty just because it is well ordered. Worship is a thing of the spirit whether much or little form is used.

Even the Society of Friends, which professes freedom from ritual, holds to established ways of doing things. In traditional Quaker meetings, the faithful gather in a particular place at a particular time. Quaker elders sit on a bench facing the people. The worshipers witness as they feel moved by the Spirit; or the meeting may proceed in complete silence. Dismissal is usually signaled by the handshake of two elders. Public worship is ritualistic to the extent that it expresses itself in customary ways.

Ritual, of course, has it attendant dangers. The trend today is to emphasize liturgy unduly. Worship can only be impoverished when it is so restricted by liturgical forms that it suppresses free charismatic expression. Form, however good, can be stressed to the point where it stifles corporate spiritual initiative and ultimately deadens the spirit it was intended to encase. The human tendency is to attach absolute values to acts of worship, with form degenerating into mere formality. Every age can testify to the fact that, for many people, perfection in performance of the rite has yielded the chief religious satisfaction. On the other hand, no act of worship can ever be merely formal if it is done of right intention.

Principles Governing the Order of Worship

If public worship is to be effective in facilitating communion between man and God, at least three principles of arrangement need to be kept in mind: the principle of unity of progress toward a climax; the principle of alternation; and the principle of proportion or balance.

1. *Unity of Progress.* Except on special occasions, the practice of unifying the service around one idea or mood is a questionable one. In his Yale lectures on preaching, Nathaniel Burton speaks strongly against that kind of worship service that wearies by its repetitious presentation of the same idea: "The first hymn sounds it—and all the hymns. The Scriptural lessons must be selected to carry it on. And each succeeding prayer must be full of its flavors."[1] He points out that the notion of many, that all things must "chime" about the sermon, is not provided for in the great historic liturgies, whose exercises move on as acts of worship in themselves.

A service that is dominated by one central idea achieves unity by uniformity, but it may in the end leave many unsatisfied. The more desirable unity is one in which every part of the service "tones in" with every other part, without the monotony of "oneness." The preparation of a color scheme for a room does not mean that one or two colors should dominate the whole. It is for most people much more satisfying if there is some variety of colors, care being taken to see that the whole blends harmoniously.

Actually, the diversity and complexity of spiritual needs in the average congregation makes a varied approach desirable. This does not mean that the service will consist of miscellany of hymns, prayers, Scripture readings, and sermon. The kind of unity to be sought is unity of progress toward a climax.

Isaiah's vision of God in the Temple suggests this unity of movement (Isa. 6). Its several aspects may be outlined as follows:

1. *Awareness of God's presence:* "I saw the Lord . . ."
2. *Adoration:* "Holy, holy, holy is the Lord . . ."

---

1. *In Pulpit and Parish,* Yale Lectures in Preaching (New York: Macmillan Co., 1925), p. 160.

3. *Confession of sin:* "Woe is me! For I am undone . . ."

4. *Assurance of pardon:* "Thine iniquity is taken away . . ."

5. *The divine challenge:* "Whom shall I send?"

6. *The human response:* "Here am I; send me."

Dr. Thomas H. Keir, a recent Convener of the General Assembly of the Church of Scotland's Committee on Worship, and a Warrack lecturer with worship as his theme, sees a meaningful and soundly theologically based order of service in terms of three essential acts. These, he points out, constitute broadly the pattern of movement in every great liturgy of the Christian Church: Eastern, Roman, Gallican, Celtic, and Reformed. His outline is reminiscent of Isaiah's experience. In the first essential act, our humble approach to Almighty God, we acknowledge who God is, and what we are. In the second act, the Word of God is heard in Scripture and sermon. The third act, to which all else leads, is in the form of Communion or, "if there be no sacramental elements, in that diverse traffic of devotion that follows as response to the Word—the belief, adoration, thankful remembrance, oblation, intercession, and remembrance of the communion of saints."[2] Kier's threefold movement may be expressed thus: (1) The Approach, (2) The Proclamation—"Hear the Word of the Lord," and (3) The Response.

The rendition of God's Word and the Church's response constitute the theological principle upon which the order of worship is based. Since worship is our response to the revelation of God in the Word, it follows that if the prayers of thanksgiving and intercession, and the offering, are to be a true response to the Word, Scripture readings and sermon should come in the earlier part of the service.

---

2. Thomas H. Keir, *The Word in Worship* (London: Oxford University Press, 1962), pp. 40-42.

In the formative days of the Church, the Scripture lections preceded the prayers and the offering,[3] a procedure still commonly observed in Reformed churches.

The more popular way in present-day Protestant worship calls for the prayers of intercession and thanksgiving and the offering to come *before* the sermon. Here the service concludes with sermon, hymn, and benediction. In support of this arrangement some hold that preaching is the true climax of worship, that God should have the last word. And of course in the dialogue between God and man, God's word always has the priority. But God speaks that man may respond. Man's total response, as already intimated, comes naturally toward the end of the service.[4]

2. *Alternation.* Within the broad pattern of worship, what is happening? Ideally, a twofold movement—an alternating rhythm—is in operation. God speaks and man responds. Christian worship is a dialogue between God and man. From concentation on God and the things of God, the worshiper moves to concentration on self. It is this ascending—descending action that makes worship a fellowship.

This alternating current operates from one act of worship to another. For instance, in Scripture reading and sermon, God is speaking to man; and in prayer and song, man essentially is addressing God. This recurring rhythm of vision and response not only operates from one act of worship to another, but it also functions involuntarily *within* these acts themselves. Although it is possible to distinguish the two movements in the dialogue of worship, it must be remembered, as S. F. Winward remarks, that such distinctions have relative, not absolute, validity.

---

3. Gregory Dix, *The Shape of the Liturgy* (London: Dacre Press, 1945), p. 455.
4. At the end of this chapter, an order of worship service is presented, suggestive of both points of view.

> Intellectually the two movements may be distinguished; in the experience of worship they are closely interwined and often merged. A hymn, for example, is a response, a spiritual sacrifice offered by the worshipper to God. It may also at the same time be used by God to address the worshipper. . . . The two movements are woven together, like the warp and woof of a garment.[5]

Insofar as the arrangement of the several parts of worship is concerned, an order of service is never to be built according to a precisely or mechanically alternating pattern. But attention given to the matter of balance between these alternating movements will do much to save worship from being austerely objective on the one hand, or suffocatingly subjective on the other.

3. *Proportion or Balance.* The service is to be ordered so that no part of it shall be unduly sustained. In general, let there be a proportionate amount of time given to each movement, and no more. Neither the music nor the sermon should usurp the time that belongs to the other parts of the service.

Addenda

The people should be encouraged to engage in prayer and meditation during the prelude.

The Call of Worship, or Scripture Words, should be said from memory.

The appropriate note after the Call to Worship is one of adoration and praise. A hymn of praise near the beginning concentrates attention on God and has a unifying effect on the congregation.

To begin the service with an Invocation is to call attention to man rather than to God. An Invocation is sometimes used just before or after the first hymn.

---

5. S. F. Winward, *The Reformation of Our Worship* (London: Carey Kingsgate Press, 1964), pp. 14-15.

Making announcements relating to the life and work of the church need not impair the dignity of the service. They should not, however, be unduly emphasized. Maxwell feels that the most unaffected position for these is just before the sermon, or immediately preceding the hymn before the sermon.

Ushers may carry the offerings to the minister, who will place them on the table.

The Doxology sometimes comes after the Offering.

After the sermon, an Invitation may be given to any who wish to respond to God's Word by profession of faith or by renewing of obedience to Christ.

The minister is to identify himself with every act of worship.

It is to be remembered that no one order of worship is always right, all others being at fault.

An Order of Worship

Prelude
Call to Worship
Invocation
Hymn of Praise
Prayer of Confession, followed by Words of Assurance
Old Testament Reading
Anthem or Gloria Patri
New Testament Reading
Affirmation of Faith
*(Children's Message)
**Prayers of Thanksgiving, Petition, and Intercession,
    followed by the Lord's Prayer
*(Announcements)
**Offertory
Doxology
Prayer of Dedication
Hymn
Sermon
Hymn
*(Invitation to Commitment)
Benediction
Postlude

Optional
**May come after the sermon*

5

The Word in Worship

The Word of God is of the very essence of worship. It is God at work in self-revelation. He comes in Scripture, sermon, and sacraments. The present chapter speaks briefly concerning the first two. In so doing it also calls attention to the Christian Year and the Creed, the one a framework for the expression of the Word, the other the people's response to the proclamation of the Word. The sacraments are taken up in a later chapter.

The Reading of the Scriptures

In the worship of the early Church there were many readings from both Testaments. By the end of the fourth century these were reduced to three—one from the Old Testament and two from the New—an Epistle and a Gospel. The last reading was always from a Gospel, the people standing meanwhile. Since the Bible revelation is a unity, there should customarily be readings from both Testaments. They may be separated by the Gloria Patri, an anthem, or a hymn, but hardly by another major act of worship.[1]

---

1. Major acts such as the prayer of confession, the general prayer, and the sermon. Among the more or less movable or variable elements are the doxology, the Lord's Prayer, and the several kinds of special music.

Because worship is man's response to the saving acts of God, the Bible—the record of God's redemptive action—should be read in the early part of the service. The praise, prayer, and offering of the people will then constitute a true response to the Word.

In these days when Bible reading is for most people confined to the church service, there is something to be said for the minister's following a sequence of readings for a year, designed to cover the major emphases of the Bible. Where there are two or more readings in the morning service, the practice might be followed in one of them. The setting forth of a coordinated view of the Bible will provide not only a balanced diet of Scripture truth, but it will be a means of delivering a congregation from being subjected unduly to the preacher's favorite passages.[2] The worship books of most churches contain lists of readings following the pattern of the Christian Year.

Preaching may conform more or less to a lectionary, or not at all. The minister will profit by using a lectionary as a frame of reference, keeping in mind the principle of flexibility in relation both to his choice of Scripture readings and sermon themes. With this appraoch, the total result may well be more satisfying. The preacher may want to compile his own lectionary for a given year in conjunction with certain areas of Bible study he plans to pursue in his preaching ministry.

When its rendering is accurate and its meaning clear, the Authorized, or King James, Version of the Bible stands unrivaled for purposes of public worship. It is not only one of the greatest monuments of English literature, but in providing a sense of unity and continuity to the Christian life it is without peer as a medium of corporate devotion. For pulpit use it still stands first in the affections of the people. If a passage is obscure in the Authorized Version,

2. For an outline of the Christian Year as commonly observed see pp. 58-61 of this chapter.

there is justification for reading it in a modern translation. But why forsake the more familiar version if the portion in question is already clear? The readings should normally be from the pulpit Bible, dedicated to this purpose.

Men are to be encouraged to listen for the voice of God in Scripture and in sermon. The bidding is, "Hear the Word of God!" As Keir puts it:

> Listen hard, for at any moment God may address you, in such a way that you experience that leap of imaginative understanding which is belief, that kindling of the will which is Christ's love in you, that obedient sense of belonging which is faith.[3]

To emphasize the need of careful listening, it has been customary to preface the Scripture reading with a brief introductory sentence, as for example:

> Hear the Word of God (or, Hear the Old Testament lesson) as it is recorded in (book), the ___ chapter, beginning at the ___ verse.

At the close of the first reading, one may say in time-honored fashion:

> Here endeth the reading from the Old Testament.

Or he may simply say, "Amen."

After the final Scripture reading, a word such as one of the following may be used:

> Blessed are they who hear the Word of God and keep it.

> Lord, to whom else should we go? Thou hast the words of eternal life.

> May God bless to us the reading from His holy Word, and to His Name be glory and praise. Amen.

There is no point in saying at any time: "May God *add*

---

3. Thomas H. Keir, *The Word in Worship* (London: Oxford University Press, 1962), p. 3.

His blessing to the reading of His Word." The blessing is *in* the Word.

In the public reading of the Scriptures some men seem to think *they* are addressing the congregation, forgetting that it is *God* who is speaking to both preacher and people. Said James Denney of a brother minister: "He never reads the Scripture as if he had written it: he always reads it as if he were listening to a Voice."

Although it is important for purposes of communication that the minister in reading recognize the presence of the congregation, his eyes, nevertheless, should be upon the text, lifting them only occasionally, at a convenient break in thought. Certainly one should avoid the habit of periodically raising his eyes in a jack-in-the-box fashion to look at nothing in particular.

That church is indeed fortunate whose minister reads well. It was John Wesley who said: "Many a congregation ought to pay its minister *not* to read the Scriptures." And one nearer our own time complained: "I do not know anything that is worse done in the Church today than the reading of the Bible by preachers."[4] The wise pastor will rehearse his readings before entering his pulpit. Following the ancient Jewish custom, qualified laymen may on occasion be called upon to read the lessons.

The Sermon

The sermon is the Word of God in a derivative sense. It seeks to interpret Scripture in terms understandable to contemporary man. When rightly understood, preaching is an act of worship. In many pulpits today, preaching seems to be regarded as something outside the context of worship, as though the two were mutually exclusive. Divorced from worship, preaching becomes moralistic or intellec-

---

4. G. Campbell Morgan, quoted by Ian Macpherson in *The Burden of the Lord,* p. 142.

tualistic and results in a loss of awareness of God's presence. Actually, the proclamation of the Word is the heart of worship. "Real preaching," says James S. Stewart, "is an encounter with God in Christ, of the very essence of worship."[5] Its whole business, George Buttrick writes, is the "bequeathing of a sense of God."[6] No worship service is complete without it. "Where the Word of God is not preached, it is better neither to sing, nor to read, nor to meet for worship."[7]

God is always man's deepest need. Here is how a spokesman for the laity expresses it:

> The layman goes to church because he hungers for God through Jesus Christ. Theology will not do it. Nice literary style will not do it. But divine love will do it, and the task of the minister, as we laymen see it, is to work into his sermons a warmth, a devotion, a deep conviction, a passion that will strongly draw them toward God through the grace of Jesus Christ.[8]

Surely, preaching at its highest occurs when God's presence becomes so real that the preacher himself almost drops out of the consciousness of the people. Dinah Morris in George Eliot's *Adam Bede* remarks with true insight: "Moses never took any heed what sort of a bush it was that was burning—he saw only the brightness of the Lord." And the Scot, John Brown of Haddington, is said to have preached with such fervor that the skeptic David Hume once commented, "He preaches as if Jesus Christ were at his elbow."

---

5. *The Christian Advocate,* 28 April 1960, p. 9.
6. George A. Buttrick, *Jesus Came Preaching* (New York: Charles Scribner's Sons, 1951), p. 139.
7. Martin Luther as quoted in J. J. von Allmen, *Worship: Its Theology and Practice* (New York: Oxford University Press, 1965), p. 145.
8. Wilbur La Roe in *Monday Morning* (a magazine for Presbyterian ministers, United Presbyterian Church), 27 February 1956.

If the vision of God through the medium of the proclamation of the Word in Scripture and sermon is of the very essence of worship, reverent listening is also a vital part of worship. Asks Spurgeon, "What can more truly be described as worship than hearing the Word of God as it demands to be heard, with faith, with reverence, with penitence, with personal application, with self-dedication, with abandonment of the soul to God our Saviour?"

When one stops to consider that a Sunday sermon can acquaint us with but a very small part of the vast stretch of God's truth, heart and mind must be open to its reception. Even the weakest preacher will say some things worth hearing. Genuine interest on the part of the hearer, not only in the sermon but in every act of worship, lends support to him who is striving to bring the truth to men. Many a worthy preacher has left church defeated because of men's indifference to the truth preached. What divine indictment must fall on him who remains manifestly indifferent to God's Word!

Our response to encounter with God through preaching may well be rich and varied. We listen in hush of spirit for and to His voice, and the result is encouragement, counsel, and correction. Some burden is to be carried, some new task assigned, some act of self-denial imposed. And we cheerfully assent. This, too, is worship of a high order.

If evangelical Christianity seeks to improve its service of worship, such improvement must never be at the expense of the pulpit ministry. The preaching function must never be allowed to suffer from the elaboration and embellishment of worship strategy. Indeed, the more spiritually mature among us, who regard the sermon time itself as a potential worship experience, will hardly feel the need for multiplying symbols and ceremonies.

An addendum to this brief word on the sermon may not be amiss. If the sermon is to mediate God to the people, if it is to evoke among them the spirit of worship, the preacher dare not slight the preparation of next Sunday's sermon. With what scrupulous care did the priest prepare himself and the sacrificial offering for the service of the Temple! The approach to God was awesome in its detail. Though we are free from the yoke of an elaborately prescribed ritual, we are to remember that God has not changed. In our sermon-offering we are to give Him our best. Said David, "Neither will I offer burnt offerings unto the Lord my God of that which doth cost me nothing" (II Sam. 24:24).

The Christian Year

The Christian Year, which developed out of the life and experience of the Church, provides a framework for the presentation of the Gospel. It sets forth progressively the great acts of God in the redemption of the world through Christ, and calls forth the proper response of the Church to the same. Since it focuses on major teachings of the Christian faith, its observance can save both minister and people from narrowness of theological perspective. Without being encumbered by a full catalogue of special days, the evangelical Church can conserve the essential values of the Christian Year by recognizing its main elements. The first half, for most Protestant bodies, lasts from Advent through Pentecost; the second half begins with Trinity Sunday and continues to the beginning of Advent.

(THE FIRST HALF)

Advent. "The Season of Expectancy" begins on the Sunday nearest November 30 (four Sundays before Christmas) and continues until Christmas Eve. The period is one of preparation for Christ's birth and calls for self-examination and penitence. Some traditional Advent themes: The Holy Scriptures; John the Baptist as the forerunner of Christ; and Christ's Second Coming.

Christmastide. "The Season of the Nativity" lasts twelve days, from December 25 to January 6. Christmas Day probably dates from the fourth century A.D. There is no way of determining the exact date of Christ's birth. First called "Christ's Mass," the term *Christmas* did not come into general use until the twelfth century. Preaching emphasizes the good news of the Incarnation.

Epiphany. "The Season of the Evangel" begins on January 6 (Epiphany Day), the thirteenth day after Christmas, and ends with the advent of Lent. This season commemorates the manifestation of Christ to the Gentiles. The word *Epiphany* is derived from the Greek *epiphaneia* (i.e., "manifestation"). The variable date of Easter means that Epiphany season may comprise from five to nine Sundays. Epiphany themes include the visit of the three wise men, Christ's baptism by John, the first miracle, and other events in the early life and beginning public ministry of our Lord. Evangelism, world missions, and human brotherhood are also emphasized during this time.

Lent. "The Season of Renewal," following Epiphany, begins on Ash Wednesday and continues forty days, not including Sundays. (The Lord's Day is traditionally a day of gladness.) The season, associated with Christ's forty-day fast in the wilderness of temptation, embraces six Sundays and ends on Easter Eve. It is a time of penitence and spiritual discipline. The term *Lent* is from the Old English *lenckten,* meaning "the spring." It referred originally to the lengthening of the days in spring.

Ash Wednesday, coming forty weekdays before Easter, is the first day of Lent. It derives its title from Old Testament times when "sackcloth and ashes" symbolized repentance. According to ancient practice, on this day the Roman Catholic priest, in preparing the kneeling penitent for Communion at Easter, marks his forehead with the ashes of palm branches consecrated the previous year. The last two weeks in Lent, beginning with Passion Sunday and Palm Sunday respectively, are known as Passion Week and Holy Week. Maunday Thursday (*Dies Mandati*) is so-called because it commemorates the institution of the Lord's Supper. Good Friday recalls the day of our Lord's Passion. The Lenten season ends officially at noon on the Saturday following Good Friday.

Easter is "The Season of the Resurrection." Easter Sunday is the oldest and greatest festival of the Christian Year. From the beginning, the fact of Christ's resurrection has been central in the Church's faith and preaching. The Council of Nicea in A.D. 325 ruled that Easter should be celebrated on the first Sunday after the full moon following the vernal equinox. The date varies between March 22 and April 25. The Season includes Easter Day and six more Sundays, the last of which is called Ascension Sunday. (Ascension Day actually falls on the Thursday previous.) Sermon themes deal with the Resurrection and the post-Resurrection appearances of our Lord.

Pentecost (Whitsunday), "The Day of the Holy Spirit," falls on the fiftieth day after Easter and commemorates the day when the Holy Spirit came upon the disciples in Jerusalem. It is generally considered the birthday of the Christian Church.

(THE SECOND HALF)

Trinity Season, "The Season of the Full Manifestation," begins on Trinity Sunday, the Sunday after Pentecost, and lasts until the beginning of Advent. It embraces from twenty-two to twenty-seven Sundays, depending on the date of Easter. Sermon themes relate to the Church's mission in the world and man's response through commitment to God.

Kingdomtide. "The Season of the Kingdom of God on Earth" is being promoted by the National Council of Churches as a subseason within Trinity Season. It continues for thirteen or fourteen Sundays, from the last Sunday in August to Advent. Its emphasis is upon the spiritual nature of Christ's kingdom and the social implications of the Gospel.

The Creed

There is something to be said for the congregation's reciting the Creed, which is really a shorthand statement expressing the Church's affirmation of the teachings of the Word. Not only does the practice help bind the people to their faith and to the great historic past of Christianity, but also it has an emotional and a unifying value for a congregation. In an age of shifting theological values, it emphasizes Biblical doctrine.

The Apostles', the Nicene, and the Athanasian creeds constitute the three great historic confessions of the early Church. The expression "the Creed" commonly denotes the Apostles' Creed. For several reasons, Christian believers formed the habit of reciting the tenets of their faith when they met together for worship. Doctrinal controversy and the growth of heresy served both to shape a statement of faith and to make its public recitation necessary. Persecution played a part in its development; for Rome required everyone to sacrifice to the emperor as to a god. In the light of contemporary needs, some churches have formulated their own creedal statement.

Inasmuch as the Creed expresses the Church's affirmation of the teachings of the Word, its rightful place in the service is either after the readings from the Scripture or at the end of the sermon. "It is a contradiction of the free nature of the Word which is to be proclaimed when in worship we come forward with the confession of faith before the proclamation takes place."[9]

9. Ernest Fuchs, "Proclamation and the Speech-Event," *Theology Today* 19 (1962): 342.

6

Prayer in Worship

The house of God is the house of prayer, for prayer is at the heart of worship. It is the Christian's "vital breath, his native air." In every act of public worship we are seeking communion with God. Understood aright, praise, Scripture reading, and sermon are all forms of prayer. But our concern at the moment is with prayer as we commonly speak of it—in expressions of thanksgiving, confession, and supplication, in which we address God directly.

At the outset, we are to remember that public prayer is not private prayer. Much confusion has resulted from failure to recognize the difference. Private prayer is between oneself and God. Public prayer, though addressed to God, is also spoken to be heard and understood by men; for it is actually the people's prayer. When the minister expresses primarily his own personal needs, aspirations, and desires, the people may listen but they will hardly join in.

The role of the congregation during prayer is never one of passive listening; it is always one of active participation. The minister praying is not only the spokesman of the people but the prompter of their prayers. Public prayer may be likened to a triangle. One ascending line represents the minister addressing God; the base line, the people listening; and the other ascending line, the people responding.

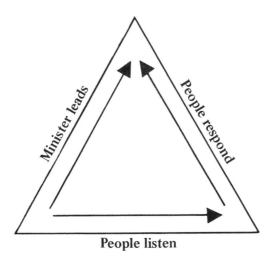

People listen

Pulpit prayer has sometimes been referred to as the shabbiest part of the morning service. All the other phases of public worship have come in for their full share of criticism, but apparently prayer is considered above censure.

Whether it be public or private, prayer should represent our best effort both in substance and form. Its intention must be of utmost sincerity, its language in keeping with the worship of God. He who on Sunday morning would seek to lift the people into conscious communion with God through prayer—surely a most difficult undertaking—cannot afford to approach his task without due preparation. The measure of his public praying will be conditioned by his own habit of private prayer. Blessed is the congregation whose pastor spends much time in the secret place! There will be times under his leadership when the people will find themselves transported into God's presence.

The best preparation for leading in public prayer comes at long range. Attesting to the fact is the injunction in *The Directory for the Worship of God*, adopted by the Presbyterian Church (U.S.A.) in 1788:

> By a thorough acquaintance with the Holy Scriptures, by reading the best writers on the subject, by meditation, and by a life of communion with God in secret, he ought to endeavor to acquire both the spirit and gift of prayer.[1]

Maxwell advises the leader in prayer to steep himself in the language of the Psalms: "A full and familiar knowledge of the Psalter will give extemporaneous prayer the directness, dignity, beauty, and appropriateness that should properly characterize prayer."[2] Familiarity with the classic prayers of the Bible will chasten the taste and mold the style of pulpit prayers. It will also be profitable for the preacher to study the great historic prayers of the Church, to catch their devout spirit, and to suffuse his mind with their felicitous phraseologies.

Insights gained in pastoral visitation will help keep the minister's prayer close to the heartbeat of the people. He can hardly pray amiss who has a sympathetic understanding of the varied circumstances under which men and women face life, who has knowledge of their hopes, enthusiasms, and frustrations. He who takes stock of the daily life of his people will not likely be found uttering prayers that bear little relation to their lives and interests.

As part of the long range preparation of prayer, the young preacher will profit by submitting to the discipline of writing suitable prayers, giving attention to the main elements of prayer, to freshness of thought and language, and to the orderly setting forth of his ideas. To avoid falling into the habit of employing stereotyped, private forms of thought and phraseology, he may keep in the prayer section of his file a variety of phrases from Biblical prayers. These could be sorted out under "salutations," "thanksgiving and praise," "confession," "petition," and "intercession."

---

1. Chapter V.
2. W. D. Maxwell, *Concerning Worship* (London: Oxford University Press, 1949), p. 53.

Attention must be given to "immediate" preparation. One should "think through" beforehand the substance of the several parts of his pulpit prayer. To leave the content entirely to the inspiration of the moment could mean the omission of significant aspects of prayer and the neglect of vital human needs and concerns.[3] Let it be remembered, moreover, that the grace of the Spirit is given not less in the preparation for prayer than in the actual occasion of prayer.

The Several Kinds of Prayer

The Invocation. The invocation is a humble calling upon God to assist us in our offering of worship. It is not an invitation to God to be present. We know that God is everywhere and always present. Many of the historic collects are excellent examples of this type of prayer. Because of its brevity, a pastor's own Invocation should be carefully prepared.

The General, or Main, Prayer. The expression "pastoral prayer," so often used in connection with public worship, is surely a misnomer. For it suggests the prayer of the pastor. As formerly intimated, prayer in worship is the prayer of the people, normally led by the pastor. In times past, this general prayer consisted of five elements: adoration, thanksgiving, confession, petition, and intercession. In recent years there has been a tendency to divide the prayer into two or more sections, allocating them to different parts of the service, a custom common in Scotland. The move is no doubt a reaction to the practice of the minister's praying over-long at the time of the general prayer, and partly in recognition of the fact that prayer stands to gain in effectiveness when its several elements receive the prominence of discreet, separate placement.

---

3. See "Prayer Reminders" in *Appendix B.*

Adoration, or an invocation including adoration, and the prayer of confession may come early in the service. The general, or main, prayer, coming later, would comprise thanksgiving, petition, intercession, and on occasion commemoration of the faithful departed. The Lord's Prayer is a climax in the movement of worship, and may properly come at the end of the general prayer.

Adoration. In the prayer of adoration, God is adored in the persons of the Father, Son, and Holy Spirit. Prayer expressing adoration seeks to recognize God—overwhelming in majesty, shrouded in mystery, and tenderly gracious to the sons of men. Adoration is a state of mind compounded of wonder, righteous fear, and love. It expresses the homage of the creature to the Creator; it is giving to the Lord the glory due to His name. Adoration is the primary element in Christian worship; it gives objectivity to the whole. Our "most fundamental need, duty, honor and happiness," says Friedrich von Hügel, "is not petition, nor even thanksgiving . . . but adoration."[4]

Thanksgiving. If in adoration we think of God because of who He is in Himself, in thanksgiving we remember Him for what He is and does in relation to ourselves. Praise seems to have been the prevailing mood in the New Testament Church. "In early Christian prayer, praise and thanks predominated. Worship in Jerusalem is described as a 'praising of God' (Acts 2:46-47). The prayers that Paul devotes to thanksgiving outnumber those of petition."[5]

Confession. Confession belongs to a full act of Christian worship, and that for at least three reasons. (1) The adoration of God for who He is, leads to the realization of our

---

4. von Hügel, *Essays and Addresses* (New York: E. P. Dutton Co., 1939), p. 224.
5. A. B. Macdonald, *Christian Worship in the Primitive Church* (Edinburgh: T. & T. Clark, 1934), p. 98.

creatureliness and to our making humble confession. The saintliest of men are quick to acknowledge their short-comings and failures before God. Such recognition helps keep men humble and alert to their utter dependence upon divine grace. (2) The Church cannot escape involvement in the sins of society. As Christians we identify ourselves with our "separated" brethren. Nehemiah thus identified himself (Neh. 1:6-7). (3) Confession is central in the Lord's Prayer.

If confession is a separate prayer, it comes near the beginning of worship, often following a psalm or hymn of praise or an invocation. Because it is the prayer of the people, it may be said by all. If the hymnbook contains no suitable prayer of confession, one may be inserted in the church bulletin. If confession is a part of the main, or general, prayer it comes after adoration and thanksgiving.

Following confession comes some form of Scriptural assurance of pardon, without which the prayer of confession is incomplete.[6] The condemnation that often results from self-examination may bring only unrelieved gloom unless the minister brings assurance of God's forgiveness through Christ. This moment may well be a climactic one for some sin-burdened soul.

Petition and Intercession. The two terms are not always held to be mutually exclusive. The distinction here used seeks to make one subjective and the other objective; i.e., we petition for our own needs and we intercede for the needs of all men everywhere. Intercession should follow an orderly arrangement—such as prayer for the world and its needs, the Church and its mission, and the poor and afflicted.

Prayer of Commemoration of the Faithful Departed. In public worship we are one with the whole Church of God,

---

6. Examples in point: Psalm 86:5; Isaiah 1:18; Romans 5:8.

militant on earth and triumphant in heaven. Remembrance of those who have gone on before is a neglected aspect of prayer in many congregations. We are ever to hold them in grateful recollection. In the Communion ritual, the prayer of commemoration often comes toward the end of the prayer of thanksgiving. An example is the following:

> We give Thee thanks, O God, for all who have fought the good fight and finished their course and kept the faith, and for those dear to us who are at rest with Thee. . . . And we beseech Thee that we, redeemed and cleansed, may stand with them before Thy throne; through Jesus Christ our Lord. Amen.[7]

The Collect. A contribution of the early Western Church, the collect—a short, concisely-worded prayer—has been used by Christians of all lands for nearly fifteen hundred years. It probably originally represented a "summing up" (*collectio*) spoken by the minister after the "bidding" prayer. Fashioned according to a definite prose pattern, it normally consists of five parts: (1) an address to the Deity, (2) a relative clause expressing some attribute of God, (3) a main petition, (4) a secondary petition related to the main petition, and (5) an ascription. A classic example of a collect comes from the seventh century:

> Almighty God, unto whom all hearts are open, all desires known, and from whom no secrets are hid: Cleanse the thoughts of our hearts by the inspiration of Thy Holy Spirit, that we may perfectly love Thee, and worthily magnify Thy holy name; through Christ our Lord. Amen.[8]

Some of the great traditional collects should be in the files of the minister.[9] He who occasionally sets himself to the

---

7. *The Book of Common Worship* (Presbyterian Church, U.S.A., 1946), p. 43.
8. Gregorian Sacramentary, Seventh Century.
9. The current *Book of Common Prayer* of the Protestant Episcopal Church contains sixty-two collects dating from A.D. 1000, in addition to forty-four later ones of which twenty-one were composed before 1549.

task of composing a collect will find the experience rewarding. The invocation, the prayer for illumination, and the offertory prayer sometimes assume this form. The worship manuals of some communions offer a different collect for each Sunday of the Christian Year (i.e., "Collects for the Day").

The Litany. Used from the fourth century, the litany is a form of responsive supplication said by minister and people. It may express praise, penitence, petition, or other worship attitudes. The leader offers a number of brief petitions, after each of which the people make a short, often fixed, response in kind, as in the opening lines of the following litany of general supplication:

> O God the Father, Creator of heaven and earth:
> Have mercy upon us.
> O God the Son, Redeemer of the world:
> Have mercy upon us.
> O God the Holy Ghost, Sanctifier of the faithful:
> Have mercy upon us.
> O holy, blessed, and glorious Trinity, one God:
> Have mercy upon us.[10]

Prayer for Illumination. The reading or the preaching of the Word is often preceded by a brief invocation, asking God to open minds and hearts to His Word, as for example:

> Almighty God, in whom are hid all the treasures of wisdom and knowledge; open our eyes that we may behold wondrous things out of Thy law; and give us grace that we may clearly understand and heartily choose the way of Thy commandments; through Jesus Christ our Lord. Amen.[11]

The Bidding Prayer. This is another type of ancient prayer. Here the minister prompts the people to pray for

---

10. *The Book of Common Prayer* (The Protestant Episcopal Church, 1928), p. 54.
11. *The Book of Common Order* (The Church of Scotland, 1940), p. 59.

specified needs, one by one, allowing a short period after each "bidding" for the people to respond silently. The minister may end with an expression of confidence in God's having heard the prayers. This kind of prayer approach helps broaden the people's prayer interests and makes for greater congregational participation in the service of worship. On occasion, the prayer of intercession may take the form of a bidding prayer.

Offertory Prayer. This brief prayer sometimes comes before, but more frequently after, the offering has been received. It is the custom in some churches for the people to stand after the offering and sing the Doxology, at the conclusion of which a short prayer of dedication is said by the minister.

The Lord's Prayer. The prayer that Christ taught His disciples is the most familiar of all prayers and too often the most abused. The manner in which some ministers hurry their congregations through the prayer can render its recitation a frustrating experience indeed. Evangelical Christianity sees no virtue in merely "repeating" prayer. When the Lord's Supper is not celebrated, the Lord's Prayer normally comes as a climax at the end of the other prayers.

Prayer Following the Sermon. The prayer after the sermon may ask God's blessing on the truth that has been proclaimed, or it may be in the form of a commitment; or again, it may be an ascription of praise to God.[12]

Amen. The "Amen" is one of the few Hebrew survivals in our ritual. From the beginning, in accordance with Jewish custom, it was the response of the worshiping

---

12. Examples of Biblical ascriptions: Jude 1:24-25; I Timothy 1:17; Revelation 1:5-6.

congregation, signifying their assent to what had been said. The leader's prayer was not the prayer of one in behalf of many. It was the people's collective prayer voiced by one man. And the people identified themselves with it by praying "Amen"—"So be it"—at the close. It needs to be emphasized that the "Amen" is essentially a congregational response. It should be understood that a choral "Amen" to prayer represents congregational response.

The Benediction. This closing prayer constitutes a climactic moment in the service. It should be spoken with deepest reverence, never perfunctorily or in haste. The minister will avoid giving the impression that he is a priest exercising a sacerdotal function. He is simply asking God's blessing upon the people. Biblical benedictions should be repeated exactly. The three most common are (1) the priestly (Num. 6:24-26), (2) the apostolic (II Cor. 13:14), and the covenant benediction (Heb. 13:20-21). There is no reason why one should not at times prepare his own benediction. In this closing prayer some men raise the right hand; others raise both hands, after the custom in the synagogue.

Free, or Extemporaneous, Prayer

Evangelical Christianity, with its high regard for the spontaneous promptings of the Holy Spirit, has always emphasized the value of extemporaneous prayer. This kind of prayer has the advantage of spontaneity, whereby the minister can respond both to the Spirit's promptings and to his own intuitive grasp of needs peculiar to his people.

"Free," or extemporized, public prayer does not necessarily mean unpremeditated utterance, springing directly from the occasion. On the contrary, this kind of prayer makes large demands on the minister. It calls for solid preparation of heart and mind. At long range, it derives from the spiritual intensity of the minister's own life in

God, and his intimate acquaintance with the ways of men and with the literature of devotion.

Like all other worthy practices, extemporized prayer is not without its attendant dangers. For one thing, it may inflict upon a congregation the minister's own state of mind or mood of the moment. Again, it is peculiarly open to the habit of employing the same kind of content and the same kind of phraseology from Sunday to Sunday. The "extempore" prayers of some men are but another species of "set" or "fixed" prayer. There is, too, a variety of "free" prayer that, owning no law and moving only according to the arbitrary will of the individual, is tantamount to the worst forms of ritualistic bondage. Even the heirs of the Puritans felt that the spontaneous prayers of ministers at times lapsed into a mixture of rambling repetitions and rhetorical vaporizings. And John Wesley, pietist though he was, agreed to extemporary prayers only as a supplement to the ritual of the less formal meetings of the Methodist societies.[13] "Whether is the wiser man of the two," asks Jeremy Taylor, "he who thinks and deliberates what to say, or he that utters his mind as fast as it comes?"[14]

Rightly conceived, "free" prayer has a significant place in the worship of the Church. The leaders of the Protestant Reformation used both "set" and "free" prayers, regarding the one as complementary to the other.

Silence in Worship

Evangelical worship has been negligent in the use of silence. The omission is understandable when it is remembered that the conduct of the evangelical service is dependent on the spoken word rather than on symbolic action.

13. Horton Davies, "The Contemporary Liturgical Movement," *Encounter* 20, no. 2 (1959): 259.
14. Jeremy Taylor, *Two Discourses* (London: 1682), p. 1.

But in the typical Protestant service, the human voice is heard throughout—in song, reading, prayer, and sermon. Modern man, moreover, is not at home in silence. What time he is not employed with daily tasks, he is subject to a barrage of auditory and visual stimuli—to a world of radio and television and stereophonic sound. If he should suddenly find himself in the "pre-acoustical" world, its silence would prove unnatural and disturbing. Modern man has a "horror of the pause."

Times of quietness in worship can be meaningful. The Quakers for more than three hundred years have demonstrated to the Christian world the value of constructive silence in public worship. The Roman Mass provides periods of silence during which the people follow the symbolic movements of the celebrant.

Surely we should make use of silence in an act of reverence on first entering God's house—an almost universal practice in earlier days. Our thoughts are to be of Him whose name is holy. We are to let the awe of the Almighty fall on us, with man the creature bowing in reverence before his Creator. Of course, there will be distractions: others entering their pews, the temptation to visit with the person next to you, the pressure of personal anxieties. But we must school ourselves to overcome all that would divert attention. The congregation that in the beginning gives itself to serious preparation for worship can profoundly affect the atmosphere of the whole service. To encourage reverence and devotion, something can be said for equipping pews with kneeling benches.

A short time of silence may well come during prayer, when the individual is encouraged to exercise his own initiative in communing with God. In every life there are needs that are unuttered in public prayer. Many a one will appreciate the opportunity of a few moments' waiting silently before God. The period must be brief. Even thirty seconds will seem long to some. It should be a time of directed silence. For instance, at the close of the intercessory prayer, or after the general prayer, the minister may say: "We bring to Thee at this time those who are especially upon our hearts, whose names we speak now in silence." Silence may also be effectively used by means of the "bidding prayer." Again, at the close of the service, following the benediction, the congregation, whose heads are bowed, may remain standing for a few moments of silence. Also, during the distribution of the elements at Communion, total silence can be impressive.

Addenda

In calling the people to prayer, say simply (e.g.), "Let us pray" (not "Shall we pray?").

Try to be orderly in your thinking. Do not mix the several parts of a prayer. Try to concentrate on one thing at a time.

Be specific in praise and petition.

Let your language be simple and straightforward. Be concise. Avoid verbosity.

Avoid redundancies (e.g., "Guide and direct us." "Bless each and every one.").

Avoid stereotyped, favorite expressions (e.g., "For whom we are duty-bound to pray.").

Avoid needless repetition of the names of the Deity.

Guard against an unhallowed familiarity.

Public prayer must never be a disguised address to the congregation.

Be sincere. Do not display a devotion you do not feel.

The spirit and the voice should connote reverence.

Let there be no undue self-deprecation. The Lord sees our humility.

Avoid a sectarian spirit. Remember Christ's words: "Other sheep I have which are not of this fold."

Resist the temptation to exhort or flatter.

In the course of the week, take note of particular matters that you should remember in prayer the coming Sunday.

Remember that our prayers have power and effect because they are offered "through Jesus Christ our Lord," our Advocate with the Father. The phrase is not just a formal ending to our prayers; it is the heart of all Christian prayer.

7

Worship in Song

Music is part of the Christian inheritance from the Hebrews. Old Testament references to music, both vocal and instrumental, witness to the large place it held in Hebrew life. No language is adequate to express the debt of the Christian faith to sacred song. "Religion must sing or die." Coleridge remarked that Luther did as much for the Protestant Reformation by his hymns as he did by his translation of the Bible.

The music of true worship is characterized by that dignity and restraint that belongs to reverence. It is music of a high order. Vital religion ennobles the spirit of man and makes him dissatisfied with offering to God anything short of his best.

It goes without saying that song rendered for its own sake has no place in public worship. It must never be employed merely to entertain or to call attention to itself. The music of worship is worthwhile to the extent that it glorifies God or communicates the Word that brings man into closer harmony with God. Augustine warned against the danger of making the music of worship an end in itself:

> So oft as it befalls me to be more moved with the voice of the singer than with the thing sung, I confess myself to have grievously offended: at which time I wish rather not to have heard the music.[1]

---

1. Augustine, *Confessions*, trans. Wm. Watts. vol. 2 (Cambridge: Harvard University Press, 1946), p. 169.

It was the fear of music becoming a snare that moved the Calvinist churches of Holland to dispense with organ and choir in the services.

Congregational singing has always been considered basic to the Protestant concept of worship. It is germane to the doctrine of the priesthood of all believers. The men and women in the pew must sing if they are to give expression to the deeper feelings of faith. Singing together not only inspires devotion but also has a unifying effect upon the congregation. It lifts the individual out of his isolation, identifying him not only with the body of believers locally but with all the faithful in Christ in heaven and on earth.

The congregation that lets the choir do most of its singing is surrendering one of the greatest privileges of corporate worship. As P. T. Forsyth once said,

> To leave the singing to the choir and the praying to the minister is popish. . . . Originally the choir in Romanism was the clergy. They did the singing. They didn't lead; they monopolized. But in Protestantism the congregation is the choir; the choir so-called is only the leader.[2]

Find that church where the choir inspires the people to rise to majestic heights in song, and you will find a well-filled church. Singing Christians are happy, witnessing Christians.

The custom, of ancient usage, of seating the choir with the congregation in the front part of the nave has much to commend it. The practice is still observed in English cathedrals. By thus making the choir an intimate part of the worshiping group, congregational singing is stimulated. The large attendance and the enthusiastic hymn-singing in Free-St. George's, Edinburgh, could be attributed in no small measure to the fact that the choir occupied seats in front, facing the pulpit, as part of the congregation. Placing the choir inconspicuously in a rear gallery has historic sanction. In an earlier period this was the custom in the

---

2. P. T. Forsyth as quoted in Donald Macleod, *Word and Sacraments* (Englewood Cliffs, N.J.: Prentice-Hall, 1960), p. 111.

churches of New England. It is still the arrangement in many Roman Catholic churches. Surely the choir should not be perched on high behind the pulpit, the cynosure of all eyes—a practice more in keeping with audience psychology than with Christian worship.

The main function of the hymn in the worship of the Church is the praise of God. We are faithful to the finest instincts of corporate worship when in song we give the Lord the glory due His name. Hymns, of course, function vitally in other ways. They can be a powerful testimony to the Church's faith. If there is a song that our age peculiarly needs, it is the song of triumphant Christian witness. When the Church sings its faith, its message is irresistible. There is also the evangelistic song, so mightily used of God in calling men to repentance.

Those subjective songs that deal primarily with the moods and feelings of the worshiper, worthy as they are on occasion, must not be allowed to obscure the great objective hymns of praise and thanksgiving. The content of the primitive Christian hymns that have been handed down to us by no means suggests the subjective emotional effusion typical of the religious songs of some contemporary Christian groups. Instead, it distinctly expresses praise for the saving activity of God in Christ. Hymns like "O Worship the King, All-glorious Above," "Praise to the Holiest in the Heights," and "Praise, My Soul, the King of Heaven," especially when they come near the beginning of worship, set forth the high purpose of the service and challenge men to reality in worship. Let then the first hymn be objective, calling the worshiper's attention to God. The hymn before the sermon may well be proclamatory in character, heralding some great event of the Gospel. Or it may be thematic, introducing the subject of the sermon. The concluding hymn may be one of commitment, invitation, or praise. Something is to be said for returning to the singing of psalms in worship. The Psalter, taken over from Temple and synagogue by the primitive Church, was the first hymnbook of the Christians. It has been the basis of Christian praise for more than nineteen centuries.

The understanding organist can contribute much to the spirit of worship. His playing ability is always subordinated to spiritual concerns. Prelude, postlude, and offertory voluntaries never become a vain show, distracting men's minds from the real purpose of worship. In accompanying the singing, moreover, the organ is never so loud that it drowns out the voices of the people.

Addenda

The instrumental prelude should help create the spirit of worship.

The postlude should help sustain the mood of the service.

Sentimental words and music have no place in Christian worship. The same holds true for music with a pronounced rhythm, calculated to excite human emotion.

When vocal announcement of a hymn is necessary, one may simply say: "The hymn is number . . ." Avoid expressions like: "Shall we sing number . . .?" "Please turn to number . . ." We are neither asking the people's permission nor begging of them a favor.

It is helpful to have the words of an anthem printed in the bulletin.

8

The Sacraments

A sacrament, as commonly defined, is an outward and visible sign setting forth and pledging an inward, invisible grace. The Protestant Reformers found authority in the Scriptures for two sacraments: baptism and the Lord's Supper.[1] These, and only these, they asserted, were instituted by Christ and enjoined by Him on His disciples. Most Protestant bodies have agreed with them. Of course, the fact that these two sacraments were instituted by our Lord does not necessarily mean that these are the sole transmitters of God's grace, for divine grace cannot be thus limited.

In the sacraments, the primacy of grace is emphasized. It is God who first of all does something. He is the central figure. In these simple observances, He comes to assure us that His promises are true and that they are being individualized.

BAPTISM

Scriptural Authority and Significance

In Matthew 28:19, our Lord commissions His apostles to "teach all nations, *baptizing them in the name of the*

---

1. Roland Bainton, *Here I Stand: A Life of Martin Luther* (New York: Abingdon Press, 1950), p. 137.

Father, and of the Son, and of the Holy Ghost." The apostles accompanied their first preaching with the administration of baptism (Acts 2:37-42). The Book of Acts lists nine specific instances of baptism being administered: the three thousand on the Day of Pentecost (2:41); the Samaritan converts (8:12); the Ethiopian (8:38); Paul (9:18); Cornelius (10:48), Lydia (16:14), and the Philippian jailor (16:33), together with their families; the Corinthians (18:8); and the Ephesians (19:5). Moral teaching contained in the Epistles rests on the ground of baptism (cf. Rom. 6:1-11; I Cor. 12:12-13; Gal. 3:27; Eph. 5:26; Col. 2:12; Titus 3:4-7; I Peter 3:2-22).

In enjoining baptism upon His disciples, Christ was not introducing a new religious rite or symbol. Ceremonial washing had long been practiced among the Jews as a sign of spiritual purification. Christ took the old symbol, already spiritually significant, and made of it a sacrament of initiation into the visible Church. Baptism, dispensed following repentance, was a symbol of cleansing from sin and consecration to the way of Christ. It really signified the inward grace essential to union with the invisible Church.

Infant Baptism

Regarding infant baptism, it is generally conceded that there is no conclusive historical evidence in the New Testament either for or against the practice. The right of parents to bring their children to God in the sacrament of baptism is understood to rest upon two principles: the unity of the family and the divine initiative.

The Unity of the Family. It is not unlikely that the references in Acts (16:15; 16:33; 18:8) to the baptism of "households" included children. The then-current use of the term "household" embraced all who were attached to a particular home. It is almost inconceivable that it did not in some instances include children. There can be no doubt, moreover, that Paul held the children of Christian parents as belonging to the Christian community (I Cor. 7:14). The apostle addresses these children as "in the Lord" (Eph. 6:1). It is unlikely that he would have used this qualifying phrase except of those included in the Body of Christ, into which, in Paul's teachings, baptism is the rite of entry. Certainly, children held a significant place in the ministry of our Lord, who asserted that entrance into the kingdom was conditioned by our becoming like them, and who warned against our offending them (Matt. 18:3-6). The words ". . . of such is the kingdom of heaven" (Matt. 19:14) imply the present membership of these little ones in the family of God. Peter reaffirms the Covenant solidarity of the people of God in the Old Testament when he says, "The promise is unto you, and to your children" (Acts 2:39).

The Divine Initiative. In the work of redemption, God acts first. "We love him, because he first loved us" (I John 4:19). It is neither our faith nor our repentance that merits forgiveness. Repentance and faith come as the result of God's Spirit working in us. The administration of baptism to infants testifies to this primary truth of the Christian Gospel. It is the manifestation of our helplessness; and, in a special way, it is the sacrament of God's unmerited grace. The justification of infant baptism is ultimately theological rather than historical. As B. L. Manning says, "Every time we baptize a child we declare to the world in a most solemn manner that God does for us what He does without our merit. In infant baptism, perhaps more plainly than anywhere else, God commends His love toward us in that 'while we were yet sinners,' Christ died for us."[2]

Baptism signifies that in the sight of God the child is provisionally pardoned and cleansed from sin. When he reaches the age of accountability, he must acknowledge

2. B. L. Manning, *Why Not Abandon the Church?* (London: Independent Press, 1939), p. 47.

the divine provision; and, confirming the step his parents took in his behalf, he should of his own free will claim Christ as his Savior and Lord.

God entrusts to the parents or sponsors the solemn obligation of bringing up the child in the nurture and admonition of the Lord. At some time prior to the public service, the parents are to be instructed in the meaning of this sacrament and in the responsibility it places on them—an occasion, incidentally, that may be ripe for personal evangelism.

At baptism, the Church, represented by the minister and the congregation, has its responsibility, too. For if this sacrament is the initiation into the Body of Christ, the response of faith must be that of the whole body and not just part of it. Too often we forget the congregation's obligation to the child. Here is a reason why baptism should normally be administered in the presence of all the people.

Adult Baptism

Before adults are baptized, they are to be instructed concerning the meaning of this sacrament, the nature of the Christian faith, the nature of the Church, and the privileges and responsibilities attendant upon church membership. They are to confess publicly their faith in Jesus Christ as Savior and Lord, and in the grace and power of God to forgive their sins; and shall promise, in dependence on God, to live for God and His Church.

Administration of Baptism

Although the New Testament gives little detailed information on the administration of baptism, it would seem that immersion was the common practice. Paul's reference to Christians being buried with Christ by baptism into death and raised up with Him to newness of life would seem to support this view (Rom. 6:3-5). But surely immersion was not the only method. The Greek word *baptizo* can mean either "to immerse" or "to bathe" (e.g., Mark 7:4, Heb. 9:10). It seems incredible that immersion was practiced on the Day of Pentecost when three thousand converts were baptized (Acts 2:38-41). As early as the first part of the second century, baptism by pouring was practiced by the Church.

In the New Testament, the rite was administered at various places: by the roadside, in the home, and in open places (cf. Acts 2:41, 8:36-38, 16:29-34). No uniform formula seems to have been used. Peter speaks of baptism "in the name of Jesus Christ" (Acts 2:38); Paul, of being "baptized into Jesus Christ" (Rom. 6:3); and again, "as many of you as have been baptized into Christ" (Gal. 3:27). The trinitarian formula, which has come into general use, is mentioned only once (Matt. 28:19).

Addenda

This sacrament is normally administered in church during a worship service. But at the minister's discretion it may be administered at another time and place.

Baptism is usually administered at the morning service. Infant baptism may come after the Scripture readings and the Creed, or it may be administered nearer the beginning of worship. Baptism of adults usually follows soon after the preaching of the Word.

Arrangements for baptism should not be extemporized for the occasion. There should be a permanent baptismal font, of significant size, visible to the congregation, and so placed as to suggest the unity of baptism with Communion and preaching.

The minister will normally follow the baptismal ritual of his church.

At a word of intimation from the minister, both minister and parents or sponsors proceed to the place of baptism.

Some ministers hold the child: others find it more satisfactory to let the father do so.

To the question, "What name shall be given this child?" only the Christian name is spoken.

In the act of sprinkling, the minister dips his fingers into the water and sprinkles the head of the child, using the Trinitarian formula (Matt. 28:19). Using this formula does not call for three sprinklings.

It is well for the people to stand while the vows are being taken.

The significance of baptism should be dealt with in the context of a sermon on another Sunday rather than elaborated upon at the time of baptism.

THE LORD'S SUPPER

Significance

As defined earlier, a sacrament is an outward and visible sign setting forth and pledging an inward and spiritual blessing. The question arises: How are these two related? The church of Rome teaches that in the Mass, the sacramental elements themselves generate this grace to the recipient, and that they do so by virtue of some quality in them apart from any spiritual activity on the part of the recipient. It is believed that when the elements are consecrated by the priest, they are mysteriously changed into the actual body and blood of Christ (transubstantiation). Christ, therefore, is held to be *physically* present on the sacramental occasion. The Mass is considered a reoffering of Christ as man's propitiatory sacrifice.

The Reformers repudiated the idea of the Mass as an objective sacrifice repeating the work of Calvary. They taught that the sacrament of the Lord's Supper was a thankful commemoration of the sacrifice Christ made for man once and for all. It brought to them not only the impact of a remembered person but also the assurance of Christ's continuing presence with them. They, too, believed in the real presence of Christ at the Supper, but to them it was essentially a *spiritual* presence. Each differed as to *how* Christ was present. Zwingli, who is generally credited with holding only to the memorial aspect of Communion, taught that Christ is spiritually *with,* not *in,* the elements: that "in the Supper the participant does truly, sacramentally, and spiritually receive the Lord's body and blood."[3] Both Luther and Calvin believed that Christ was present in some unique way in the bread and wine, and that in some miraculous manner the elements convey grace to the participant. Luther taught that the body and blood became fused with the elements (consubstantiation).

Although Calvin, like Zwingli, did not believe that the real presence of Christ was enclosed in the bread and wine, he nevertheless held that the sacrament carried an "objective force" by divine appointment, that it was not simply suggestive or commemorative, not just a sign deriving its significance from the mind of the beholder. Pressed to explain just how Christ is present, Calvin confessed it to be a mystery too sublime to be expressed.[4]

The evangelical position on the Supper is based upon the Reformed tradition, which is in turn that which the Reformers took to be the New Testament position. This sacrament is believed to be more than a memorial to God's love set forth in Christ. It is also regarded as a means appointed by Christ not for purposes of instruction but to demonstrate the living presence of Christ in the lives of the participants and to lift them into new communion with Him. The occasion is held to be chiefly a fellowship between the soul and Christ.

Our Lord at the Supper is both the Giver and the Gift. *He* invites us to *His* table to partake symbolically of that which *He* has provided. Christ, it is believed, is spiritually present to the faith of the believers as the elements are to

3. Nathaniel Micklem, ed., *Christian Worship* (London: Oxford University Press, 1936), p. 137.
4. John Calvin, *Institutes of the Christian Religion,* vol. 2 (London: Westminster Press, n.d.) p. 684.

their outward senses. The bread and wine are understood to be instruments of grace just as the Bible, prayer, or a hymn may be said to be grace-bearing. It is believed that the Spirit uses the elements to awaken faith, without changing their substance or investing them with some force to make them other than signs or symbols. The grace that comes to us is not something transmitted through the elements. The Spirit does not have to be mediated to us. He comes directly. At this sacrament, which dramatizes what God did for man through Christ, we are confronted with "the presence, the memory, and the hope all in one."[5]

Evangelicals, then, believe in the real presence of Christ at the sacrament—a spiritual presence, not in the elements but in the rite as a whole. Most evangelical bodies in the United States repudiate the teaching that the real presence is localized at the Communion table. The New Testament Church had no designated "place," no "holy place," spatially conceived, to celebrate the Lord's Supper. Christ's presence was understood to be a mystical presence, at once "in the midst" and in the heart of the believer. Nor do evangelicals commonly believe that the presence of Christ at the Supper is different from His presence at other parts of the service. Whereas one occasion may render men more receptive to His presence than another, Christ, it is believed, is ever present to the apprehending faith of the believer. To try to localize God in a set of circumstances or in an object is foreign to New Testament teachings. Brother Lawrence had so schooled himself in the receptive attitude that he could say, "In the noise and clatter of my kitchen, I possess God in as great tranquility as if I were upon my knees at the Blessed Sacrament."

After examining all Eucharistic rites, ancient and modern, Eastern and Western, Archbishop Yngve Brilioth, the

5. Donald Baillie, *The Theology of the Sacraments* (New York: Charles Scribner's Sons, 1957), p. 106.

Swedish theologian, concluded that a full statement of the doctrine of the Supper must include at least five aspects: commemoration, thanksgiving, fellowship, sacrifice, and mystery.[6] Later Biblical scholarship has added one more aspect, the eschatological, with particular reference to the celebration of the Messianic banquet in eternity.

First, the Supper is a *memorial* to the death of Christ for the sins of the world. In partaking of the bread and wine we remember His body that was broken and His blood that was shed for our salvation. "This do in remembrance of me."

Secondly, it signifies *thanksgiving.* "Jesus took the cup and gave thanks." As Christians we offer unto God our thanksgiving and praise for what Christ accomplished in our behalf. It is said of the first Christians: "And they, continuing daily with one accord in the temple, and breaking bread from house to house, did eat their meat with gladness and singleness of heart" (Acts 2:46).

Thirdly, it represents *fellowship.* At the Lord's table we experience spiritual union with Christ, with one another, and with the vast communion of saints on earth and in heaven. We are one body in Christ (cf. I Cor. 10:17). Partaking of food together symbolizes the fact that we share with one another the life that we derive from God.

Fourthly, it stands for *sacrifice.* In no sense is the Supper a substitute for or a repetition of the one Sacrifice made on Calvary. "For Christ also hath once suffered for sins, the just for the unjust" (I Peter 3:18). Nor does any sacrifice on man's part belong to the essential meaning of this sacrament. Of course, in the light of Christ's atonement, man offers himself as a living sacrifice to God. But man's sacrifice is in response to the sacrament, which symbolizes God's gift.

Fifthly, the Lord's Supper is a *mystery.* This fact of

---

6. Yngve Brilioth, *Eucharistic Faith and Practice: Evangelical and Catholic,* trans. A. G. Herbert (London: Society for the Promotion of Christian Knowledge, 1930), chap. 2.

mystery underlies the whole service. There is the mystery of Christ's real presence. Those early disciples experienced the continuing presence of the living Lord. It is clear His presence was not confined to sacramental occasions. Luke records that on one occasion He became known to two disciples "in the breaking of bread" (Acts 24:35b). There is also the mystery concerning how Christians are united to Christ, to one another, and to the vast communion of saints. The Church is not just an association but "a Body, even the Body of Christ."

Christian worship is man's response to a twofold presentation of the Word: the Word spoken in Scripture and in sermon; and the Word acted in the sacraments. One medium presents Christ in words, the other in deeds. The second confirms the first. The Word acted is the sign and seal of the Word spoken. As Goethe once said, "The highest cannot be spoken, it can only be acted." In Christ, God acted and spoke at the same time.

Because it is the Word that gives significance to the elements, Communion should not be separated from the reading and preaching of the Word. In the primitive Church the sermon was essentially a part of Eucharistic worship. Said Calvin, "The true ministration of the Sacrament standeth not without the Word." It was in medieval times that the sermon came to be omitted—"a degenerate step linked with the multiplication of said masses and the incompetence and illiterateness of the clergy."[7] It took the Reformation to restore the sermon to its proper place. *The Companion to the Book of Worship* (United Methodist Church) advises: "It is sound and right that every celebration of this sacrament should include a lesson or lessons from the Holy Scriptures and a sermon."[8]

---

7. W. D. Maxwell, *Concerning Worship* (London: Oxford University Press, 1948), p. 68.
8. W. F. Dunkle, Jr. and J. D. Quillian, Jr., eds., *The Companion to the Book of Worship* (Nashville: Abingdon Press, 1970), p. 56.

It is not generally held that the "preaching service" is necessarily impoverished when it takes place apart from Communion. To insist otherwise would seem not only to make of the Supper an essential instrument of mediation between God and man, but it would also in all probability have the effect of relegating the spoken Word to a subordinate position in the service. It expresses the same thing in a different way. Although it may not be regarded as necessary to every service, it is usually felt that Communion loses something vital when it is celebrated apart from the "Liturgy of the Word." The preaching of the Word is a direct preparation for the administration of the sacrament.

Communion must never be observed as a kind of appendage to the regular service. The entire morning service is a unit, a complete whole. All else—hymns, Scripture, prayers, and sermon—should have some bearing on the Communion. That the entire service be not prolonged unduly, pre-Communion prayers and the sermon may need to be curtailed; without, however, giving the appearance of haste.

Administration of the Lord's Supper

Specific procedures in administering the Lord's Supper vary among denominations and even among churches of the same denomination. During the singing of the hymn before Communion it is customary for the minister to remove the cloth covering the elements. According to almost universal practice from earliest times, the minister himself communicates first, in both kinds. This priority is not because of deference to ministerial status. The Lord being the host, the minister, symbolically speaking, takes the bread and wine from His hand. In so doing he is an example to the people. Moreover, he who would be the means of nourishing others must first himself be divinely nourished.

If another assists, he is served immediately after him

who presides. It is becoming the practice in some churches to serve the choir after the clergy, in recognition of their service as a ministry of song.

Quiet, unobtrusive organ music is sometimes played while the elements are being administered. Some people, however, find music at this time to be distracting and prefer to observe Communion in silence.

When another minister assists, historic practice suggests that the minister in charge distribute the bread and the assistant the wine, and that the former be responsible for all the details, such as removing the linen cloth and delivering the elements to the assistant.

In handling the elements both hands should be used. By reciting from memory the parts of the ritual in question, one can avoid the necessity of holding the service book.

In the Reformed tradition it is still the common practice for lay elders to bear the elements to the people, seated in their pews—a practice in all probability in accord with the most ancient tradition.[9] This custom, abandoned in the fourth century, was later restored, particularly by Zwingli at Zürich. Today, the more widespread and equally acceptable procedure is for the congregation to go forward to participate, usually in a kneeling position. This is the general practice in Methodism.[10]

In some churches, it is the custom for each member to hold the elements in his hand until everyone is served, then all partake together. The practice, known as "simultaneous communion," has little to recommend it. It can be unnatural and crippling to the spirit of devotion.

It is important that the Church standardize its procedure in the observance of Communion according to the

9. J. J. von Allmen, *Worship: Its Theology and Practice* (New York: Oxford University Press, 1965), p. 299.
10. But at the discretion of the minister, the people may be served in the pews. See Dunkle and Quillian, *Companion to the Book of Worship,* p. 15.

general pattern set forth by Christ on the night of the Last Supper. But to pay undue attention to a pattern of external acts could reduce the whole to an empty ritual. The spirit that we bring to the sacrament is infinitely more important to the meaningfulness of the occasion than is a precise reproduction of the original action. As Fiske says:

> When we think of the uncounted billions of followers of Christ who during the past nineteen centuries have observed this simple Sacrament of Communion, with greater or less elaboration of liturgy or in its original simplicity, it is quite possible that it has bound together more human lives in the fellowship of worship than any other symbolic ceremony in the long history of religion in this world.[11]

Should the Lord's Supper be administered to children? Opinion here is divided. Von Allmen asserts that the whole ancient Church admitted children to Communion. In the West the practice was discontinued, partly because of the definition of the dogma of transubstantiation, with its disconcerting implications concerning the misuse of the elements. On children and communion von Allmen has this to say:

> It is false theologically to make the admission to Communion depend on confirmation of baptism, a practice which depreciates the sacrament of baptism. We must restore to the children the right to communicate, and we must insist on it so much the more because children are unable to claim for themselves a right which is theirs. . . . If we wish to maintain the exclusion of children from communicant life, then we must also exclude them from baptism.[12]

Surely, however, Communion should not be administered to small children, who have no understanding of its significance or who have no sense of personal commitment in the matter.

---

11. G. W. Fiske, *The Recovery of Worship* (New York: Macmillan Co., 1931), p. 168.
12. von Allmen, *Worship*, pp. 187-188.

Some Protestant ministers have been following the Roman Catholic practice of serving Communion in connection with the marriage ceremony. In view of the distinctly corporate nature of the Lord's Supper it would seem that a special Communion for the bride and groom would be ill-advised. When the sacrament is observed, all present are to be invited to participate. A couple may be encouraged to attend a Communion service shortly before or after their marriage.

May the sacraments be administered by the laity? Speaking as a Congregationalist, Nathaniel Micklem answers the question thus:

> Stress is properly laid upon the priesthood of all believers; but the true Congregational principle seems clear that except in cases of necessity it is the minister who should celebrate the Christian sacraments; for our God is a God of order, not of anarchy. Ministers have been called out of the Church under the guidance of the Holy Spirit in virtue of the spiritual gifts entrusted to them; they are ordained to be ministers of the Word and Sacraments. As a matter of order therefore (not of validity), laymen should not administer the Sacraments unless under exceptional circumstances the Spirit should so direct.[13]

Frequency of the Supper

With respect to the frequency of Communion it would seem from Acts that the rite was observed weekly in conjunction with the reading and preaching of the Word. "They continued stedfastly in the apostles' doctrine and fellowship, and in the breaking of bread, and in prayers" (Acts 2:42). "And upon the first day of the week, when the disciples came together to break bread, Paul preached unto them" (Acts 20:7).

In the ancient Church there is no intimation of Sunday worship being celebrated without the Eucharist. As stated earlier, both Luther and Calvin believed that the Lord's Supper should be celebrated at least weekly. Luther con-

---

13. Micklem, *Christian Worship,* p. 254.

tinued to regard the sacrament as the central act of worship. For Calvin it was the natural as well as the traditional climax of the service. But, hindered by the civil authorities in Geneva from carrying out his intention of weekly Communion, Calvin had to resort to Zwingli's custom of quarterly observance, a practice to be widely adopted in England and Scotland, and one that served in the end to subordinate the sacrament to the sermon by making the latter the climax of worship.

For both John and Charles Wesley, the Supper was the norm of worship. The first rule of the Methodist Bands was that each member be at the Lord's table every Sabbath.[14] When he arranged the service for Methodists in America, John Wesley advised that the Lord's Supper be administered every Sunday. *The Worshipbook—Services* (published jointly by the Cumberland Presbyterian Church, the Presbyterian Church [U.S.], and the United Presbyterian Church [U.S.A.]) urges frequent celebration of the Lord's Supper, even as often as each Lord's Day.[15]

Those who come to the defense of less frequent Communion insist that we do greater justice to the power of the sacrament when it is observed less often. Many feel that the Sunday-to-Sunday preaching of the Word meets the ethical, intellectual, and spiritual needs of the people more adequately than does a weekly observance of the Supper. There is always the danger of the frequent repetition of an act deadening the force of that act.

The Communion Ritual

The minister will follow the Communion ritual of his denomination. The arrangement of the ritual can, in gen-

---

14. J. E. Rattenbury, *Vital Elements of Public Worship* (London: Epworth Press, 1936), p. 77.
15. *The Worshipbook—Services* (Philadelphia: Westminster Press, 1970), p. 34.

eral outline, be traced back many centuries. It is as follows:

Communion hymn

The Invitation

The Prayer of Confession (if it has not
  been said in the early part of the service)

The Words of Institution

The Prayers of Consecration

The Distribution

The Prayer of Thanksgiving

The Hymn

The Benediction

An Order of Worship for the Communion Service follows on page 96.

An Order of Worship for the Communion Service

Prelude

Call to Worship, or Scripture Sentences

Hymn of Praise

*Prayer of Confession, followed by
    Words of Assurance by the minister

Prayer for Illumination

Old Testament Reading

Gloria Patri

New Testament Reading

The Sermon

**The Creed

The Prayer of Intercession

The Offertory

Communion Hymn

The Invitation

The Words of Institution

***The Prayer of Consecration

The Distribution

The Prayer of Thanksgiving, followed by
    the Lord's Prayer to be said by all

Hymn

Benediction

Postlude

* The Prayer of Confession may follow the Invitation.

** The Creed may be recited after the Scripture readings.

*** Immediately following this, the practice of many ministers is to break the bread (i.e., the Fraction) and raise the cup, reciting the appropriate Scripture words.

9

The Church Wedding

The practice of solemnizing marriage in church rather than making a declaration in a municipal building testifies to the fact that the contracting parties believe that their marriage is of concern to God and that His abiding blessing is essential to the success of their venture. It is felt, and here witnessed to, that transcending their own desires is a divine purpose to be worked out in their lives. Like all other services held in the church, the wedding is essentially a service of worship, dedicated to the glory of God. It is in this spirit that the service is to be conducted, in this spirit all of its materials chosen. To these ends, the minister should counsel with those about to be married. Since, in our society, marriage and family relationships are less clearly defined than in other years, the Christian minister in his role as premarital counselor has a unique opportunity to help prepare the engaged couple for at least some of the realities of the Christian marriage relationship. Areas of significance would include matters such as compatibility, Christian beliefs, the seriousness of marriage, the Christian attitude toward sex, and the setting up of the Christian home.

Preliminary Considerations

As part of the preparation for marriage, the couple should read over carefully each part of the ritual. No words of the ceremony are spoken at the rehearsal.

The minister is normally in charge of the wedding rehearsal.

The music—organ and vocal—should reflect the intent and purpose of the Christian wedding service. Music of purely secular associations is hardly in keeping with the spirit of the service. Religious songs of sentimental vintage are likewise to be discouraged.

One or two solos are sometimes rendered. If two, the first may come before and the second after the seating of the bride's mother.

For seating purposes, the ushers ask the guests entering the church if they are relatives of the bride or groom.

The parents of the bride and groom are seated in a front pew, the bride's parents to the left (facing the chancel) and the groom's to the right.

The groom's parents are seated immediately before the seating of the bride's mother, who is the last person to be seated before the ceremony begins.

Other relatives are seated behind the parents—the bride's on the left (facing the chancel) and the groom's on the right.

An usher escorting a lady may offer her his right arm.

After the mother of the bride has been seated, two ushers unroll (from the chancel end of the church) the aisle runner, if one is used.

Should there be a flower girl,[1] she will precede the bride and her father. At the chancel she may stand behind the maid of honor, slightly to her right.

Photographs should not be taken during the ceremony proper.

The Processional (See diagram, page 101)

Following the unrolling of the aisle cloth, the ushers are in their place at the head of the bridal party. This is the

---

1. The flower girl and the ring bearer are now less in fashion.

signal for the organist to begin the processional music. At the sound of the first few bars of music, the minister, the groom, and the best man enter by the shortest way to their respective positions—the groom at the minister's left (facing him) and the best man at the minister's right.

At the entrance of the minister, the bride's mother rises, and the congregation follows.

The ushers now begin to lead the bridal party down the aisle. If the church has two aisles, one may serve for the processional, the other for the recessional.

The bridal party proceeds at a comfortable walk, slowly and in time, left foot first, and keeping about four pews apart, except in the case of the bride walking with her father. The distance between them and the rest of the bridal party should be at least twice as long.

Bridesmaids may walk singly or in pairs. Should there be an uneven number they walk singly.

The bride usually proceeds leaning on her father's right arm.

At the Chancel (See diagram, page 101)

When the principals are in their appointed places, the minister begins by reading the preliminary statement on the nature of Christian marriage. This is followed by the charge to the couple, after which prayer may be offered. The questions of intention are then asked, followed by the giving away of the bride.

The Christian names of the bride and bridegroom may be used in place of "this man and this woman."

The reply to the question "Who giveth this woman to be married to this man?" should be, "I do." It is understood that the father, or another answering, represents the entire family of the bride. He should avoid the somewhat sentimental expression, however well-intentioned, "Her mother and I do."

After giving away the bride, the father joins the bride's

mother in the pew, and the maid of honor lifts the bride's veil and receives her flowers.

In a chancel arrangement, minister, bride and groom, maid of honor, and best man may now proceed to the Communion table or altar within the chancel, for the saying of the vows and for the ring ceremony. A kneeling cushion should be provided.

Before taking the vows, the minister may say simply: "As a seal to the vows you are about to make, give each other the right hand."[2]

The taking of the vows may be followed by the ring ceremony, the ring symbolizing the covenant entered into. It is given by the best man to the minister, who returns it to the groom for placement on the third finger of the bride's left hand. In a double ring ceremony, the minister, receiving the ring from the maid of honor, gives it to the bride, who places it on the third finger of the groom's left hand.   Following the ring ceremony the minister shall ask them to join their right hands for the pronouncement of the declaration of marriage.[3]

The couple kneels for prayer and the Lord's Prayer (recited also by the people).

The service ends with the benediction, followed by the recessional.

The Recessional (See diagram, page 101)

At the close of the ceremony, the bride turns to the maid of honor to receive her bouquet. She then accepts the groom's right arm, and together they lead the recessional.

In the recessional the bridesmaids may pair together or

2. After the groom's vow, the couple loose hands. Then before saying her vow, the bride with her right hand takes the groom by his right hand.
3. In some traditions the declaration of marriage is read after the couple rise from saying the Lord's Prayer.

ushers may pair with the bridesmaids, each offering his right arm.

After the recessional, the head usher escorts the bride's mother, the father following. A second usher escorts the groom's mother.

The minister may remain in his position until the relatives retire from the pews and then dismiss the congregation with upraised hands. Or an usher may come to the front of the center aisle and dismiss the people with a like gesture.

DIAGRAMS OF ARRANGEMENTS

The Processional
(Read from the bottom up.)
Bride and Father
Flower Girl (if any)
Maid of Honor
Bridesmaid(s)
Bridesmaid(s)
Ushers (2)
Ushers (2)

At the Chancel
Minister

Bridesmaid   Maid of Honor   Bride   Groom   Best Man   Bridesmaid

Usher   Usher   (Flower Girl)   Father   Usher   Usher

The Recessional

(Read from the bottom up.)
Usher Usher
Bridesmaid Usher
Bridesmaid Usher
Maid of Honor Best Man
Bride Groom

Processional for a Double Wedding

(Read from the bottom up.)
Younger Bride with Father or sponsor
Maid of Honor of younger Bride
Bridesmaids of younger Bride
Senior Bride and Father or sponsor
Maid of Honor of senior Bride
Bridesmaids of senior Bride
Ushers paired according to height

ARRANGING THE SERVICE

Organ Prelude

Seating of guests

Lighting of candles (if any)

Groom's parents seated

Brides's mother seated

Aisle cloth unrolled

The Processional

The Ceremony[4]

The Recessional

Brides's parents ushered out

Groom's parents ushered out

Congregation dismissed (at signal from minister or usher)

---

4. The officiating minister usually follows the wedding ritual of his church.

An Experiment in the Church Wedding *

To free the modern wedding of secular trappings and make it a more worshipful experience, one pastor, with the cooperation of a young couple about to be married, prepared what he felt was a wedding ceremony designed to reflect the intent and purpose of the Christian wedding.

A folder, presented to each guest on arrival at the church, was entitled "An Introduction to the Ritual of Worship for the Marriage of Miss Mary Smith and Mr. John Jones." It contained not only the order of service but an explanation of the occasion:

> You have been honored by the invitation of a young man and woman to share in one of the happiest and holiest moments in their lives. You are their guest, and you are also the guest of this church. The wedding ceremony is not just a social occasion with a religious touch thrown in. It is a service of worship from beginning to end, in which vows are made, prayers are offered, and a blessing is given. It is in fact the celebration of a very sacred rite. You are present in order to participate, always inwardly and sometimes audibly in this act of worship.

As the wedding party entered the church, the choir, in the front part of the gallery, led the congregation in the singing of the processional hymn, "Praise, My Soul, the King of Heaven." The ritual indicated that the congregation was also invited to stand and sing the hymn. Another departure from tradition was the processional arrangement of the wedding party. The minister led the way, followed by the flower girl and the ring-bearer. Then came four bridesmaids, each escorted by an usher. The maid of honor was accompanied by the best man. The bride was escorted by the bridegroom.

---

* For the substance of this write-up (including the quoted excerpts), I am indebted to Allen B. Reesor, "A Wedding Can Be an Act of Worship," *The Christian Advocate* 7, no. 13 (20 June 1963), copyright 1963, The Methodist Publishing House. Used by permission of the publisher.

The congregation sat after the final amen of the processional hymn. The bride's father stepped out of his pew and stood behind the bride.

The marriage ritual was the traditional one, except for an introduction, which called for the reading of I Corinthians 13. To encourage congregational participation, the folder stated:

> As the ceremony proceeds, members of the congregation are encouraged to continue to be in the spirit and attitude of worship. No married person present should miss the opportunity of giving thanks to God for his own marriage, and of silently renewing his own vows that are now being given for the first time by others. No guest should leave the service without praying that God's many blessings may truly rest upon this man and this woman all the days of their lives together.

The minister and the bride and bridegroom moved *into* the chancel for the pastoral prayer, which was followed by the Lord's Prayer, recited also by the congregation. The bride and bridegroom remained kneeling for the general prayer, the Lord's Prayer, the declaration of marriage, and the final blessing.

During a recessional hymn, "The King of Love My Shepherd Is," the congregation stood and sang with the choir. After the hymn the congregation was seated and the guests remained in their pews until directed to rise by the ushers. The folder contained this final word:

> We hope that you have regarded yourself as a worshiper rather than as a spectator in this service, and that you have sensed the dignity and order and beauty that can always be a part of the ceremony of marriage. You are invited to take this little folder with you as a reminder of this happy occasion. Go from this church in peace, and may the God of peace go with you always.

10

The Christian Funeral

The Nature of the Service

The purpose of the funeral service is to glorify God and to comfort the bereaved. For the Christian Church, the burial of the dead is always to be regarded as an act of worship in which the Word of God is proclaimed through the reading of the Scriptures. Whether or not there is a sermon is left open. The custom of the local community often dictates funeral procedures, not always wisely. A service consisting of Scripture reading and prayer is justified by ancient precedent. If there is a meditation it should be pastoral in aim and it should be brief. No attempt is to be made to cover up the reality of death. Offer instead the strength of the Christian faith. Scripture, prayer, and hymns should help the bereaved experience the presence and power of Christ that they may be sustained in facing the reality of their loss. The singing of hymns is always in order in the house of God. What can be more uplifting at a Christian funeral than the hearty singing of the great hymns of the faith, such as, "O God, Our Help in Ages Past," "For All the Saints Who from Their Labors Rest," "The Strife Is O'er, the Battle Done," "Look, Ye Saints, the Sight Is Glorious"? Hymns like these are both worshipful and therapeutic. It may be wise, however, to omit congregational singing if the group is small. Organ music will be the more strengthening to the bereaved if it is music with which they are familiar and which holds for them meaningful association. The people may participate not only in the singing of hymns but also in the reciting of the Lord's Prayer and in responsive reading. The entire service at the church normally lasts from twenty to thirty minutes.

The Place

In these days of funeral homes, which accommodate not only all kinds of Protestant groups but also adherents of other religions as well as those of no religious faith, there is sometimes little to distinguish the funeral service of evangelical Christianity from the rest. When practicable, the proper place for a Christian funeral service is the home church of the deceased. It is here no doubt where the deceased was admitted into the fellowship of the believers, where he attended Sunday school, where he was joined in marriage, and where he partook of the Lord's Supper. Sometimes, however, practical considerations may require that a funeral be held in a funeral establishment or even in a private home.

Procedure

As the minister precedes the pallbearers and the family down the aisle toward the chancel,[1] the congregation rises as a gesture of respect for the deceased and sympathy for the family. The pallbearers customarily sit to the left, facing the minister, and the family and relatives to the right.

At the close of the service, the principals leave the church in the order in which they entered. The minister stands, head uncovered (weather permitting), near the

---

1. If the remains are already lying in state, the minister precedes the family and the relatives.

door of the hearse until the casket is in place. He then proceeds to his car to lead the cortege to the cemetery.

At the cemetery he again leads the pallbearers and family to the place of interment.

At the words of committal, "Earth to earth, ashes to ashes . . . ," let him cast on the casket a little of the good earth.

Addenda

When possible the family should call the minister before death occurs, that he may perhaps have opportunity to pray with the dying, and with the family.

On the occasion of death, the minister visits the family to offer sympathy and to help in any other way he can.

The situation calls for wisdom and understanding. At such a time, the minister's presence may contribute more than his words.

If he is approached about the funeral service, he will seek to comply with the wishes of the family, at the same time keeping in mind the proprieties of the Christian funeral service. At such a time he may see the need of advising distraught loved ones regarding funeral expenditures. A casket so expensive that it brings financial distress to the living is hardly the way to honor the dead.

Instead of overspending on flowers, consideration might be given to putting the money to use in a way that both honors the deceased and blesses the living.

The practice of displaying the body in an open casket in the church is a questionable one. Much may be said for having the casket closed before the service begins and for keeping it closed. The attention of the mourners is to be directed toward spiritual, transcendental realities rather than to earthly remains. A viewing of the remains at the undertaker's parlor on the eve of the funeral may meet the need.

Should the funeral service be given an evangelistic emphasis, such concern will best be served if expressed indirectly, and in a spirit that accords with the solemn realities of death and the hereafter.

In Christian worship there is no justification for eulogizing the dead. "It is a denial of our faith if we feel called upon to list the greatness of the one departed as if we were giving God some basis for mercy."[2] This is not to say that an appropriate word of commendation should not on occasion be offered. Even so, praise should always reflect God's grace rather than man's goodness. The Christian funeral service commends the departed to God, and calls upon the bereaved to lift their thoughts above their concern for the earthly body to a new relationship within the communion of saints.

No other rite or ceremony should be permitted to intrude upon the service conducted by the church.

Except under unusual circumstances, funeral services should not be held on Sundays. The practice may interfere with the regular services of the church. Moreover, undertakers and their assistants should not be required to work unnecessarily on Sundays.

One of the minister's greatest services may be performed by his calling on the bereaved after the day of the funeral, when all the friends are gone. Indeed, one's responsibility to the sorrowing family may well continue during the days, and perhaps weeks, after the funeral. The time involved will depend on the particular circumstances of the family.

If there is a cremation, the ritual is almost the same as that of the service in the church. Instead of saying, "We commit this body to the ground," one says, "We commit his remains to their last resting place."

---

2. W. F. Dunkle, Jr. and J. D. Quillian, Jr., eds., *The Companion to the Book of Worship* (Nashville: Abingdon Press, 1970), p. 99.

An Order of Funeral Service

Scripture Sentence(s)
Hymn
Prayer
Scripture Readings
(Brief Meditation)
Prayer, and the Lord's Prayer
Hymn
Benediction

The Service at the Cemetery

Scripture Sentence(s)
Words of Committal
Prayer
Benediction

Appendix A

Involvement in Worship

CHILDREN IN WORSHIP

Insofar as possible, families should worship together. The habit can contribute much to the spiritual solidarity of the home. Children who reasonably early form the habit of church attendance are more apt to continue the practice.

Where nursery facilities are available during the worship hour, the mother of small children should make use of them. If a child in church becomes fretful during the service, the wise parent, seated near an exit, will immediately remove him. Some parents have retained a disturbed child for the duration of the service to "break his will," seeking thereby to intimidate him into submission, a procedure that is hardly fair to preacher and people, or to the child himself.

Older children in church should be encouraged to participate in the service. They should join in the hymns and in other acts of worship, such as responsive reading, the creed, and the Lord's Prayer.

It will help make the children feel even more a part of the service if the minister takes time to address a brief message to them. This usually comes in the early part of the service, is three or four minutes long, and is followed by a children's hymn sung by the whole congregation. If some feel that a children's message during the regular service might lower the tone of worship, it may be said that this is by no means the case in the experience of those Scottish churches where the custom of speaking to the young at the morning service has long prevailed. If the minister loves children and has regard for the proprieties of the pulpit, the children's address can only strengthen the spirit of worship. If it is feared that a message to the young would lengthen unduly the morning service, surely a careful planning of the service would obviate this concern. In the interest of conciseness of style alone, many a morning sermon could without serious loss be curtailed by three or four minutes. Planning for the children should engage the same scrupulous care as planning for adults. The children's message will hold the attention of the adults also. In fact, the minister may on occasion be somewhat disconcerted on discovering that his discourse to the young elicited more congregational response than did the morning sermon. Sometimes it takes a talk to children to demonstrate to adults some of their own misconceptions of truth.

He who doubts his ability to hold the interest of children needs to remember that most preachers possess greater power in this regard than they have ever exercised. They have simply never devoted themselves to the task.

Here a word may be said about the "Junior Church." Does the usual contemporary format of the "Junior Church" prepare the children for participation as worshipers in the regular services of the church? The watering-down of adult practices in the form of small-dimension worship centers, chalk-talk moralizings, attention-getting demonstrations, and other miscellaneous expedients may prove interesting and informative, but one wonders if in the end they play a significant role in the child's development in the worship of God. If we keep in mind the integration of the spirit and practices of the "Junior Church" with the worship of the church, the goal should be more nearly achieved.

Addenda (Practical considerations)

The content of the message must capture the child's attention.

Let one significant truth stand out.

The message should as a rule emphasize positive truth.

Since the child's mind responds best to the pictorial, the language should be concrete rather than abstract.

To help create interest in the Bible, try to make its episodes and characters come to life for the child.

Like our Lord, the wise storyteller will often seek to reveal spiritual insight in a situation or object familiar to our common life.

The message should be spoken conversationally, with simple directness.

Remember that children do not like being "talked down to."

Let there be a minimum of moralizing. It is better to let the story carry its own lesson.

The success of the talk to children is more dependent upon the spirit and personality of the speaker than is the case with the sermon for the adult.

The message may be in the form of a brief story, a simple explanation, a dialogue, or perhaps a convincing statement of "reasons why" one ought to adopt a certain attitude or pursue a certain course.

The children's message, followed by a children's hymn, may well come after the Scripture readings, in which case the customary "hymn before the sermon" might be omitted.

Suggested Topics for a Series of Brief Talks to Children

New Testament Stories Retold

Old Testament Stories Retold

Parables from Nature

Stories of Great Hymns

"Endless Line of Splendor" (Missionary Heroes)

Moments in the Lives of Great Christians

The Lord's Prayer

How We Got Our Bible

Symbols in the Church

Great Moments in Church History

The Meaning of Worship

Leaders of the Reformation

Stories from Everyday Life
Questions Children Ask

THE MINISTER IN WORSHIP

The chief aim of any religious service is to provide the people with a definite experience in God. To this end the minister is committed. In seeking to bring about a corporate worship encounter, the man of God engages in a dual role: in leading the people in worship he remembers that he, too, is a worshiper. He is to identify himself with every act of the service, not just with those functions in which he assumes active leadership. He should join in the singing of the hymns and be as attentive when the choir is singing as he expects the people to be attentive when he is preaching. After a lifetime of pulpit experience, John Oman remarked, "As to what makes a service worship, more and more I come to think that it depends on worshiping with the congregation, and not merely conducting their worship."[1]

The high seriousness of his calling suggests what manner of man the leader in worship ought to be. Be it humbly yet firmly said that the Christian minister, notwithstanding his human limitations and imperfections, is the divinely commissioned revealer of God to man. He speaks as the oracle of God. "As though God did beseech you by us," says the apostle, "we pray you *in Christ's stead,* be ye reconciled to God" (II Cor. 5:20).

No other factor in public worship will inspire more reverence in the pew than the spirit and deportment of the minister himself. In conducting the service, he should be prompt yet never hurried, at ease yet never casual, cheerful without being frivolous, warm without being sentimental. Principal Shairp's description of John Henry Newman ascending the pulpit stairs at St. Mary's, Oxford, seems remote from our generation of ministerial activism: "From the seclusion of study, and abstinence, and prayer, from habitual dwelling with the unseen, he seemed to come forth that one day of the week to speak to others of the things he had seen and heard."

Let the preacher beware of an affliction that plagues too many of today's pulpits, the disease of "clerical verbosity." The "uninterrupted garrulity" of the Protestant ministry in our day is a source of irritation to many. "There's hardly an occasion," says one critic of today's pulpit, "when the preacher doesn't feel called upon to make a few remarks . . . making an announcement, giving out a hymn, taking up an offering, opening up an occasion for ministerial chat."

In appraising the ministerial role in the conduct of public worship, one might ask himself, "Does my conduct of the service evidence concerns such as these?":

— adequate preparation for each part of the service, with a sense of balance and proportion in choice and arrangement of the materials of worship?

— personal strength and vitality in the administration of the entire service?

— freedom from obtrusive self-display in talent, mannerism, and dress?

— sympathetic understanding and appreciation of the needs of the congregation? "I sat where they sat" (Ezek. 3:15).

— leadership that reflects truly the spirit of worship?

THE OPEN DOOR

Much can be said for keeping God's house open daily that all who will may enter for prayer and meditation—a practice that prevailed in Britain and on the Continent in the early days of the Reformation. The locked door during the week is hardly a credit to the Christian Church. When Jesus said, "My house shall be called the house of prayer," He surely did not intend that it should be used for this purpose only a few hours one day a week. In England toward the close of the last century the struggle to keep the churches open was so successful that today it is the exception to find a church locked on a weekday. One cannot of course close his eyes to the very real danger of theft and vandalism. The risk, however, can be reduced by keeping smaller objects of value under lock and key on weekdays. In the urban or inner city church, where the congregation is sizeable, it may be possible to employ for modest remuneration a retired pensioner as caretaker. Some elderly but active members might welcome an opportunity to serve the Lord by devoting a few hours a week to this work.

On weekdays, members of the congregation and others should feel free to enter the church for prayer and meditation. In praying thus alone, one may learn to withdraw himself from the turbulence of daily life and push aside distractions that so readily populate the mind, seeking only to wait on God. The pursuit calls for self-discipline. Where the practice does not prevail, the people will profit by some instruction on how to use these times of quiet creatively. A few tangible aids may be given them, such as reading portions from devotional parts of the Bible or other inspirational literature. A stanza or two from a familiar hymn often serves to quiet the mind and set the attention Godward.

It is not that prayer and meditation in the quietness of the sanctuary is to be a substitute for private devotions in the home. Yet in God's house, with table, pulpit, and lectern reminding us of God's presence, and in a setting long hallowed by sacred memories, one may at times find it easier to pray. In this place, too, designated primarily for corporate worship, the individual is reminded of the fact that he is one of a family, a part of the royal priesthood of believers. This awareness cannot but have a salutary effect upon him who prays.

Why should not the minister himself on a weekday go to the house of God to pray? There he sees the pews that are occupied regularly by the faithful, and he is inspired to pray for the people according to their needs. His habit will be a source of blessing and inspiration to all.

It is expedient also that as families we spend some time, though brief, in preparation for the service of public worship. An appropriate time would be the eve of the Sabbath. Thereby, both old and young are more likely to go to the house of God with anticipation. "Strength and beauty are in the sanctuary"—for all who come expectantly.

Appendix B

Worship Resources

THE CALL TO WORSHIP

The Lord is in his holy temple: let all the earth keep silence before him.

—Hab. 2:20

I was glad when they said unto me, Let us go into the house of the Lord.

—Ps. 122:1

This is the day which the Lord hath made; we will rejoice and be glad in it.

—Ps. 118:24

116

O magnify the Lord with me, and let us exalt his name together;
For great is the Lord, and greatly to be praised.

−Ps. 34:3; I Chron. 16:25

I will lift up mine eyes unto the hills: from whence cometh my help?
My help cometh from the Lord, who made heaven and earth.

−Ps. 121:1-2

Wait on the Lord: be of good courage, and he shall strengthen thine
heart: wait, I say, on the Lord.

Ps. 27:14

Draw nigh to God, and he will draw nigh to you.

−James 4:8

The Lord is in his holy temple: let all the earth keep silence before
him. Surely the Lord is in this place. This is none other than the
house of God, and this is the gate of heaven.

−Hab. 2:20; Gen. 28:16-17

Let all the earth fear the Lord: let all the inhabitants of the world
stand in awe of him.

−Ps. 33:8

O come, let us worship and bow down; let us kneel before the Lord
our Maker. For he is our God, and we are the people of his pasture,
and the sheep of his hand.

−Ps. 95:6-7

O give thanks unto the Lord, for he is good: for his mercy endureth
forever. O that men would praise the Lord for his goodness, and for
his wonderful works to the children of men!

−Ps. 107:1,8

Who shall ascend into the hill of the Lord? Or who shall stand in his
holy place? He that hath clean hands, and a pure heart; Who hath
not lifted up his soul unto falsehood, And hath not sworn deceitfully.

−Ps. 24:3-4

Seek ye the Lord while he may be found; call ye upon him while he
is near: let the wicked forsake his way, and the unrighteous man his
thoughts: and let him return unto the Lord, and he will have mercy
upon him; and to our God, for he will abundantly pardon.

−Isa. 55:6-7

Behold, I stand at the door and knock [saith the Lord]: if any man hear my voice and open the door, I will come in to him, and will sup with him, and he with me.

—Rev. 3:20

The Lord is nigh unto all them that call upon him, to all that call upon him in truth. He will fulfill the desire of them that fear him; He also will hear their cry, and will save them.

—Ps. 145:18-19

My soul longeth, yea, even fainteth for the courts of the Lord; my heart crieth out for the living God.

—Ps. 84:2

Our help is in the name of the Lord, who made heaven and earth.

—Ps. 124:8

The hour cometh, and now is, when the true worshipers shall worship the Father in spirit and in truth: for the Father seeketh such to worship him. God is a Spirit: and they that worship him must worship him in spirit and in truth.

—John 4:23-24

Particularly Appropriate for Evening Worship:

From the rising of the sun unto the going down of the same, the Lord's name is to be praised. Let our prayers be set forth as incense before him; the lifting up of our hands as the evening sacrifice.

—Ps. 113:3; 141:2

The day declineth, for the shadows of the evening are stretched out; But it shall come to pass, that at evening time there shall be light.

—Jer. 6:4; Zech. 14:7

It is a good thing to give thanks unto the Lord, and to sing praises unto thy name, O most High; to show forth thy lovingkindness in the morning, and thy faithfulness every night.

—Ps. 92:1-2

The Lord will command his lovingkindness in the daytime, and in the night his song shall be with me, and my prayer unto the God of my life.

—Ps. 42:8

It shall come to pass that at evening time it shall be light.

—Zech. 14:7

When therefore it was evening, on that day, the first day of the week, and when the doors were shut where the disciples were, Jesus came and stood in the midst, and saith unto them, Peace be unto you.

—John 20:19

THE INVOCATION

Almighty God, unto whom all hearts are open, all desires known, and from whom no secrets are hid: cleanse the thoughts of our hearts by the inspiration of Thy Holy Spirit, that we may perfectly love Thee and worthily magnify Thy holy name; through Christ our Lord. Amen.

—Gregorian Sacramentary, 7th Century

O Thou who art our Creator and our Friend, we bow before Thee in humble trust, craving a deeper knowledge of Thy nature and Thy will. Take away, we pray Thee, all thoughts and feelings which separate us from Thee, and help us to worship Thee in spirit and in truth. Amen.

—Charles E. Jefferson

O Lord our God, who art always more ready to bestow thy good gifts upon us than we are to seek them, and art willing to give more than we desire or deserve: help us so to seek that we may truly find, so to ask that we may joyfully receive, so to knock that the door of thy mercy may be opened unto us; through Jesus Christ our Lord. Amen.

—Book of Common Order of St. Giles' Cathedral

O Thou Holy One, who inhabitest eternity, visit us with the inward vision of thy glory, that we may bow our hearts before thee, and obtain that grace which thou hast promised to the lowly, through Jesus Christ our Saviour. Amen.

—The Book of Common Worship

Almighty God, who dwellest in light unapproachable, whom no man hath seen or can see; grant that we may know thee in him whom thou hast given to be the light of the world, our Saviour Jesus Christ, and in the joy of his gospel may worship thee in spirit and in truth.

—Hugh Cameron

O God, Author of eternal light, lead us in our worshiping this day; that our lips may praise Thee, our lives may bless Thee, our meditations may glorify Thee; through Christ our Lord. Amen.

—Sarum Breviary, 11th Century

O Lord, our merciful Father, we pray Thee to look upon us gathered here in Thy presence now, and to shed upon us as a congregation, and upon each of us individually, the helpful spirit of Thy grace, that all our thoughts and desires now may be such as Thou canst sanction and satisfy, and that in our worship we may each of us be aware that we have come into Thy presence. Amen.

—Alexander Maclaren

OFFERTORY SENTENCES

Let your light so shine before men that they may see your good works, and glorify your Father who is in heaven.

—Matt. 5:16

Freely ye have received, freely give.

—Matt. 10:8

Remember the words of the Lord Jesus, how He said, It is more blessed to give than to receive.

—Acts 20:35

Every man according as he purposeth in his heart, so let him give; not grudgingly, or of necessity: for God loveth a cheerful giver.

—II Cor. 9:7

Honor the Lord with thy substance, and with the first fruits of all thine increase.

—Prov. 3:9

The earth is the Lord's and the fullness thereof; the world, and they that dwell therein.

—Ps. 24:1

We brought nothing into this world, and it is certain we can carry nothing out.

—I Tim. 6:7

What shall it profit a man, if he shall gain the whole world, and lose his own soul?

—Mark 8:36

Upon the first day of the week let every one of you lay by him in store, as God hath prospered him.

—I Cor. 16:2

Whatsoever ye do, do it heartily, as to the Lord, and not unto men. He that giveth, let him do it with liberality; he that showeth mercy, with cheerfulness.

—Col. 3:23; Rom. 12:8

Every man shall give as he is able, according to the blessing of the Lord thy God which he hath given thee.

—Deut. 16:17

He that soweth sparingly shall reap also sparingly; and he that soweth bountifully shall reap also bountifully. With what measure ye mete, it shall be measured unto you.

—II Cor. 9:6; Mark 4:24

OFFERTORY PRAYERS

Unto Thee, O Lord, do we offer the gift of our hands and the loyalty of our hearts. Accept us with our gifts, we pray, in Jesus name. Amen. *(Minister's Service Book* edited by James Dalton Morrison.)

Graciously accept, O Lord, these gifts and so attend them with Thy favor that they may bring joy to many hearts and glory to Thy name; through Jesus Christ our Lord. Amen. (*Minister's Service Book* edited by James Dalton Morrison.)

O God, of whose bounty we have all received: Accept this offering of Thy people; and so follow it with Thy blessing that it may promote peace and good will among men, and advance the kingdom of our Lord and Saviour Jesus Christ. Amen. (*The Book of Common Worship [Presbyterian, U.S.A.]*)

Almighty God, our heavenly Father, who hast not spared Thine own Son, but delivered Him up for us all, and who, with Him, hast freely given us all things; receive these offerings which we bring and dedicate to Thee; and enable us, with all our gifts, so to yield ourselves to Thee, that with body, soul, and spirit we may truly and freely serve Thee, and in Thy service find our deepest joy; through Jesus Christ our Lord. Amen. *(The Book of Common Order of the Church of Scotland.)*

O God, the Fountain of all good; we bring to Thee our gifts, according as Thou hast prospered us. Enable us, with our earthly things, to give Thee the love of our hearts and the service of our lives. Let Thy favor, which is life, and Thy lovingkindness, which is better than life, be upon us now and always; through Jesus Christ our Lord. Amen. *(The Book of Common Order of the Church of Scotland.)*

O Lord our God, who givest liberally and upbraidest not, teach us to give cheerfully of our substance for Thy cause and kingdom. Let Thy blessing be upon our offerings, and grant us to know the joy of those who give with their whole heart; through Jesus Christ our Lord. Amen. *(The Book of Common Order of the Church of Scotland.)*

We thank Thee, O God, for the multitude of Thy tender mercies. Gratefully we bring our gifts to Thee. Accept and use them for the extension of Thy kingdom; through Jesus Christ our Lord. Amen.

Most gracious God, of whose bounty we have all received, accept these our gifts. Help us to show our gratitude to Thee by yielding unto Thee ourselves and all we possess; through Jesus Christ our Lord. Amen.

O Lord, we offer these our gifts for the work and witness of Thy Church. Take them, we pray, and multiply their usefulness, even unto the ends of the earth. Amen.

THE ASCRIPTION

Now unto the King eternal, immortal, invisible, the only wise God, be honor and glory for ever and ever. Amen.

—I Tim. 1:17

Now unto him that is able to do exceeding abundantly above all that we ask or think, according to the power that worketh in us, unto him be glory in the church by Christ Jesus throughout all ages, world without end. Amen.

—Eph. 3:20-21

Now unto him that is able to keep you from falling, and to present you faultless before the presence of his glory with exceeding joy: to the only wise God our Savior, be glory and majesty, dominion and power, both now and ever. Amen.

—Jude 24-25

Unto the God of all grace, who hath called us unto his eternal glory, . . . be glory and dominion for ever and ever. Amen.

—I Peter 5:10-11

Unto him that loved us, and washed us from our sins in his own blood, and hath made us kings and priests unto God and his Father; to him be glory and dominion for ever and ever. Amen.

—Rev. 1:5

Blessing, and honor, and glory, and power, be unto him that sitteth upon the throne, and unto the Lamb, for ever and ever. Amen.

—Rev. 5:13

Blessing, and glory, and wisdom, and thanksgiving, and honor, and power, and might, be unto our God for ever and ever. Amen.

—Rev. 7:12

THE BENEDICTION

Grace, mercy, and peace from God the Father, Son, and Holy Spirit, be with you henceforth and for ever. Amen. *(From* The Book of Common Order *of the Church of Scotland, p. 312.)*

Go in peace; God the Father, Son, and Holy Spirit bless, preserve, and keep you this day (night) and for evermore. Amen. *(From* The Book of Common Order *of the Church of Scotland, p. 312.)*

The Lord bless you and keep you: the Lord make his face to shine upon you, and be gracious unto you: the Lord lift up his countenance upon you, and give you peace. Amen.

−Num. 6:24-26

Now may the God of peace who brought again from the dead our Lord Jesus, the great shepherd of the sheep, by the blood of the eternal covenant, equip you with everything good that you may do his will, working in you that which is pleasing in his sight, through Jesus Christ: to whom be glory for ever and ever. Amen.

−Heb. 13:20-21

And may the blessing of God Almighty, Father, Son, and Holy Spirit, sustain and prosper you now and evermore. Amen.

The peace of God, which passeth all understanding, keep your hearts and minds in the knowledge and love of God, and of his Son Jesus Christ our Lord; and the blessing of God Almighty, the Father, the Son, and the Holy Spirit, be among you, and remain with you always. Amen. *(From* The Book of Common Order *of the Church of Scotland, p. 311.)*

The grace of the Lord Jesus Christ, and the love of God, and the communion of the Holy Spirit, be with you all. Amen.

−II Cor. 13:14

The very God of peace sanctify you wholly, and preserve you blameless unto the coming of our Lord Jesus Christ. Amen.

−I Thess. 5:23

Now the God of hope fill you with all joy and peace in believing, that ye may abound in hope, through the power of the Holy Spirit. Amen.

−Rom. 15:13

PRAYER REMINDERS

Praise and Thanksgiving

To Thee, O God, our Father, infinite, eternal, and unchangeable, glorious in holiness, full of love and compassion, abundant in grace and truth.

To Thee, O Christ, our Saviour, who suffered and died that we might be reconciled to God.

To Thee, blest Holy Spirit, who hath quickened us together with Christ, and hath shed abroad His love in our hearts.

We praise Thee, O God:

for our creation, preservation, and all the blessings of this life.

for Thy Word, which is a lamp unto our feet and a light unto our path.

for the everlasting riches of Thy mercy.

for the Church and Christian inspiration and instruction.

for Thy providences over us.

for the assurance that we are heirs of God and joint-heirs with Christ.

for home and loved ones.

for every evidence of the Spirit's leadings.

for Thy great and precious promises.

for assurance of life everlasting.

for Thy patience that hath borne with us.

for all that sustains our faith and makes us rich toward God.

for Thy fatherly discipline that chastens us.

for teaching us the uses of adversity.

for work to do and strength to do it.

for the work of healing in hospitals and homes.

for men and women in harsh circumstances who face life uncomplaining.

for earth, sea, and sky, and all the beauties of this world.

for the memory of Thy faithful servants, who now rest from their labors.

for the blessings we enjoy from the labors of those who lived before us.

Confession

We confess to
faltering faith in the face of obstacles.
dullness in apprehending Thy providences in our lives.
petty strivings that waste our energies.
attachment to the world and neglect of things spiritual.
failure to be true always to what we know is right.
weakness in adversity and self-sufficiency in prosperity.
taking for granted the services of others.
the sin of covetousness.
words hastily spoken.
an uncharitable spirit.
complacence toward wrongs that do not involve us, and sensitiveness
    to those that do.
insincerity in word and action.
reluctant feet and a procrastinating will.
cautious giving.
taking lightly the one talent Thou hast given us.
failure to apply to ourselves standards we demand of others.
presuming upon Thy mercy.
making small use of large gifts.
slowness in sharing the burdens of others.
complaining when we should be thankful.

Petition (for our own needs)

From the fret and fever of life, we turn aside to seek the quietness of
    Thy presence.
Lord, teach us that our highest thoughts of Thee are but dim
    shadowings of Thy transcendent greatness.
Help us to live so near to Thee that all else will appear little in
    comparison with eternal realities.
Train our minds to settled contemplation of Thee, and our lives to
    constant imitation of Thy ways.
May we be indwelt by God, the object of all love, who Himself is
    Love.
Help us to see that our smallest service is of eternal value when
    linked with Thy purposes.
Thou hast set us in a place of wonder but our vision is weak. "Lord,
    open Thou our eyes."

Grant us that spiritual far-sightedness that sees beyond the show of things.

Forbid that we should look upon the work of Thy hands, and give no thought to Thee, the Maker of all things.

May we continue in Thy way, undismayed by the inexplicables of life, undisturbed by the reverses of fortune.

Help us to remember always that darkness and light are both alike to Thee.

Open our eyes to behold Thy manifold ministries.

Grant us grace to submit to the unchangeables of life.

Give us strength to put right before self-interest.

May Thy Spirit be in our homes that they may be protected from dangers within and perils without.

Help us to realize that we are saved from nothing if we are not saved from sin.

Let not our general sense of well-being or the prosperity of our undertakings deceive us into a false reliance on our own strength.

Deliver us from the temptation to rationalize our otherwise unjustifiable conduct.

Save us from wasting our mistakes, our failures, our sorrows. Help us to use them for Thy glory.

Let Thy light burn through our excuses.

Deepen our concern for all sorts and conditions of men.

Help us, Thy children, to live in the bond of Christian unity.

Grant us the instinct to discern the essential from the nonessential, the transient from the abiding.

Teach us to bear our infirmities with cheerful patience.

Deliver us from bondage to mere *things*.

Help us to be scrupulously honest in all our business relationships.

Let us not mourn unduly for those who have "outsoared the shadow of our night."

Intercession (for others)

We pray for:

Thy Church Universal.

the Church in this land, that she may be faithful to the trust which Thou hast committed to her.

the ministry of the Word in all lands.

missionaries in the faraway corners of the earth.

Continued

all who are seeking God.
the homes of the nation.
peace among nations.
all who suffer persecution for the sake of the Gospel.
all who are lost in the way of error.
the blind, the deaf, and the dumb.
the sick and all whose lives are wasted by disease.
those in whom the pulse of life grows weak.
all who watch while others sleep.
family circles broken by death.
all who have lost the kindly light of reason.
all who are troubled by anxiety and suspense.
all who stand in the valley of decision.
all who are sorely tempted.
men and women embittered by life
victims of race prejudice.
all who are engaged in the work of alleviating human suffering.
the teachers of our children.
universities and colleges.
men and women in the armed services.
our enemies.
the poor and the underprivileged.
justice in relations between employers and employees.
those in places of responsibility in government.
missions to the Jews.

Glossary of Worship Terms

Altar—The Communion table; also called the Lord's table or the holy table.

Amen—A Hebrew word meaning "verily" or "so be it"; historically, a congregational response at the end of prayer or praise.

Anthem—A musical composition usually set to words from the Psalms or other parts of Scripture.

Antiphonal—Responsive; such as responsive reading, singing, or chanting.

Apse—A semicircular projection at the front of a church, facing the congregation.

Ascension Day—The fortieth day after Easter, commemorating the ascension of our Lord.

Ascription—A brief doxology sometimes said by the minister after a sermon or after prayer.

Baptistery—The place where the sacrament of baptism is held.

Benediction—The invocation of the divine blessing at the close of the service.

Bidding Prayer—A form of directed corporate prayer in which the leader prompts the people to pray for specific needs. Each prompting is followed by a brief period of silence.

Canticle—A hymn or song from the Bible, not including the Psalms (e.g., The Magnificat, Luke 1:46-55).

Cassock—A black gown worn under other garments.

Chalice—The cup containing the sacramental wine or grape juice used at Communion.

Chancel—That area of the church building which commonly contains the Communion table, baptismal font, pulpit, lectern, and choir.

Christian (Church) Year—A seasonal arrangement of the year focusing on cardinal points in the life of our Lord.

Collect—A short, carefully ordered prayer form usually containing a single petition.

Communion—A term for the sacrament of the Lord's Supper. Also called "Holy Communion."

Cruciform—A church building in the form of a cross.

Dossal (Dorsal)—The curtain hanging on the "east" wall of the chancel and behind the Communion table or altar.

Doxology—An ascription of praise to God.

East—The liturgical "east" is that end of the church in which the Communion table is situated.

Easter—The day commemorating our Lord's resurrection; also the season of "forty" days commemorating the same.

Ecumenical—Worldwide; in Protestantism, commonly the movement designed to include all Christian bodies in one, in recognition of the oneness of the body of Christ—the Church.

Elements—The bread, wine, and water used in the sacraments.

Eucharist—An early designation of the Lord's Supper, signifying thanksgiving.

Fraction—The act of breaking bread at Communion.

Gloria Patri—A Trinitarian doxology traditionally used after the reading from the Psalms, affirming the identity of the God of the Old Covenant with the God of the New Covenant.

Hymn—A song of praise to God; commonly, a general term for any religious song.

Invocation—The act of calling upon God to assist us in worship.

IHC (IHS)—The first three letters of the Greek word for Jesus.

INRI—The initials of the Latin inscription on the cross, "Jesus of Nazareth, King of the Jews" (John 19:19).

Lectern—A reading stand from which the Scriptures are read.

Lectionary—A list of Scripture readings following the pattern of the Christian Year.

Litany—A form of responsive supplications recited by minister and people.

Liturgy—Generally, a prescribed pattern of public worship; specifically, the order of celebration of the Lord's Supper.

The Mass—The Holy Communion of the Roman Catholic Church, so designated from the fifth century. The term probably derives from the words of dismissal, "Ite missa est."

Maundy Thursday—The Thursday of Holy Week so called because it commemorates the institution of the Lord's Supper. (Latin, *Dies Mandati.*)

Narrative (Words) of the Institution—The Scriptural account of the establishment of the Lord's Supper (Matt. 26:26-29; Mark 14: 22-26; Luke 22:17-20; I Cor. 11:23-25).

Nave—That part of the church building occupied by the congregation.

Offertory—The presentation of the bread and wine for the sacrament of the Lord's Supper; also, the giving of material gifts as an act of worship.

Pentecost—The seventh Sunday (fiftieth day) after Easter, commemorating the descent of the Holy Spirit. *See* **Whitsunday.**

Processional—An act, usually performed by choir and minister, symbolizing the beginning of public worship. A processional hymn is sung by choir and congregation as the choir moves from the narthex to the chancel.

Psalter—The Book of Psalms; or psalms arranged for devotional use.

Rubric—Directions in the ritual for the conduct of the several acts of worship.

Sacrament—An act of worship instituted by our Lord in which outward and visible symbols represent inward and spiritual grace. Protestants generally recognize two sacraments: Baptism and the Lord's Supper.

Sanctuary—In the "free" churches the term is widely used to denote the entire church building; in the Episcopal Church, that part of the church where the altar is located.

Stole—A narrow band of silk worn about the neck, signifying the pastoral office.

Surplice—A white linen vestment, wide-sleeved and knee-length, worn over a cassock.

Trinity Sunday—A Sunday honoring the Trinity and beginning the Trinity season; the Sunday after Pentecost.

Whitsunday—The day of Pentecost, commemorating the Holy Spirit's descent upon the apostles; so called from the white robes worn by the converts (catechumens) who on that day joined the church.

Worship—The response of the creature to the Creator; the act of ascribing to God supreme worth.

Index